MR. FUNKY'S
Super Crochet Wonderful

by Narumi Ogawa

MR. FUNKY'S
Super Crochet Wonderful

Narumi Ogawa

NORTH LIGHT BOOKS
CINCINNATI, OHIO
www.artistsnetwork.com

11 10 09 08 07   5 4 3 2 1

Distributed in Canada by Fraser Direct
100 Armstrong Avenue
Georgetown, ON, Canada L7G 5S4
Tel: (905) 877-4411

Distributed in the U.K. and Europe by David & Charles
Brunel House, Newton Abbot, Devon, TQ12 4PU, England
Tel: (+44) 1626 323200, Fax: (+44) 1626 323319
E-mail: postmaster@davidandcharles.co.uk

Distributed in Australia by Capricorn Link
P.O. Box 704, S. Windsor, NSW 2756 Australia
Tel: (02) 4577-3555

Library of Congress Cataloging-in-Publication Data
Ogawa, Narumi.
   Mr. Funky's super crochet wonderful / Narumi Ogawa.
      p. cm.
   Includes index.
   ISBN 13 978-1-58180-966-4 (alk. paper)
   ISBN 10 1-58180-966-2
   1. Crocheting. 2. Crocheting--Patterns. I. Title.
TT820.O33 2007
746.43'4041--dc22

35892867 8/07   2006038689

Editor: Jessica Gordon
Designer: Cheryl Mathauer
Illustrator: Dylan Haley, Type Goes Here, Inc.
Production Coordinator: Greg Nock
Technical Editor: Julie Holetz
Photographers: Adam Henry, Adam Leigh-Manuell and John Carrico of Alias Imaging, Inc.

F•W PUBLICATIONS, INC.

Acknowledgments

First of all, I'd like to thank everyone who helped Mr. Funky to grow.

I'd like to thank Ms. Jessica Gordon for being such a great editor. I learned a lot from her, and I thank her for being patient with me, too.

I'd like to thank my illustrator and good friend, Dylan Haley. It's been a pleasure working with him on this project.

Many thanks to book designer Cheryl Mathauer; technical editor Julie Holetz; and photographers Adam Henry, Adam Leigh-Manuell and John Carrico of Alias Imaging, Inc.; and also to production coordinator Greg Nock.

I'd like to give big thanks to my friend Zanna Williams for supporting Mr. Funky. I could not have completed this book without her!

And last but not least, I'd like to give big hugs and kisses to my dearest Karl Fornander and Mr. E. Rufis McGee.

Dedication

This book is dedicated to all the people who never thought they were crafty, but who want to try. And to all the funky crocheters who never found a book with both patterns and charts.

Funky! Funky! Funky!

INTRODUCTION

Mr. Funky Crochets

My first endeavor in crocheting was when I happened upon a crocheting book for southpaws. I had felt like I wasn't crafty all my life until I found something that finally spoke my language! My hope is that this book will be fun for left- and right-handed crocheters of all skill levels, as well as for knitters.

The designs in this book incorporate a sense of frivolity and flair that I gleaned from my childhood in Japan and my adulthood in Los Angeles. When I first began, I didn't know a thing about crocheting, but I was able to follow charts and eventually became comfortable with patterns. As my love of crocheting expanded, I sought out pattern books that offered new, fresh and contemporary designs. But most of the books I could find were filled with projects that reminded me of my grandmother's wardrobe. So, instead of following patterns, I began creating my own designs and experimenting with clothing and accessories

I thought would mesh with the trendsetting styles of my friends. My newfound creativity helped me to tap into the playfulness of my youth and inspired me to re-create the familiar, silly toys of my childhood.

The intent of this book is to make you feel funky and to make sure you have some fun while creating each piece. There are two parts to this book. The first section is made up of cute, quirky stuffed animals in the style of Japanese Amigurumi. Each design has step-by-step instructions including both written patterns and charts. Most of the designs can be made in one or two sittings. The second section includes a wide range of hip, wearable accessories that have been sold in upscale boutiques throughout the United States.

Perhaps it's time to break out your crochet hooks and discover (or rediscover) your crochet skills. I hope you enjoy the projects in this book.

Mr. Funky's Tips for Happy Crochet

Here are a few hints for making your crochet projects even more beautiful. If you follow these three easy suggestions, you'll always have a good time crocheting. And your animals and accessories will turn out perfectly lovable and lovely.

- First, try to make a habit of taking care of loose ends as you work. To keep loose ends from showing, always weave them back through several stitches or work over them. When ends are secure, clip them off close to your work.

- Secondly, use markers. Markers can help distinguish the beginning of each round. You can get markers from a craft store or make them with a scrap of yarn.

- And finally, check your gauge before starting a project. This is important to ensure that your finished project has the correct measurements, based on the number of stitches and rows per inch (in) or centimeter (cm). See page 109 in the Mr. Funky Wants You to Know section for more information on gauge.

AMIGURUMI ANIMALS

Mr. Funky's
Amigurumi Animals

This chapter will show you how to make sweet stuffed animals in the style of the Japanese art, Amigurumi. Typically, Amigurumi (crocheted stuffed dolls) have large, oversized noggins and cylindrical bodies. These designs incorporate original accessories to personalize your Amigurumi. You can add pom-poms or cute buttons with fuzzy or glittery yarns. You might notice that your Amigurumi enjoy wearing scarves and hats to keep them warm or need a purse for carrying their everyday necessities. Sometimes, Amigurumi can be useful to a person on the go. Check out the **Panda Bear Keychains** (see page 24) and the **On-the-Go Water Bottle Carrier** (see page 48). Your favorite valentine might enjoy **The Real Mr. Funky** (see page 28). Or if you don't have a valentine this year, the **Snazzy Stripes Snake** (see page 44) will snuggle up around your neck to keep you warm on a February night.

To construct these lovable animals, you will mainly need two crochet hooks, a larger size for increasing stitches and a smaller size for decreasing stitches. One important thing to remember when making the dolls is to leave a long tail when you finish crocheting each of the extremities and head (not the body) so you have plenty of yarn for sewing the parts together. And when you finish the face, make sure the parts are evenly placed. Is the nose in between the eyes? Are the eyes on the same row? And finally, use plenty of stuffing and distribute it evenly. A chopstick or thick crochet hook can help you fill your Amigurumi without leaving any unsightly lumps. Then make sure that each Amigurumi is tickled and squeezed when the need arises. See page 109 in the Mr. Funky Wants You to Know section for basic instructions on sewing an Amigurumi animal together.

SPECIAL NOTES

All the patterns in this chapter are worked in a continuous round without turning or joining at the end of each round, unless otherwise specified. Place a marker in the last stitch of each round to mark the end of the round.

Decrease using the following method for all the animals in this chapter, unless otherwise specified: Insert hook in next st, yo and draw up loop, insert hook in following st, yo and draw up loop, yo and draw through all 3 loops on hook.

boy and girl elephants

Unlike the stork, this pattern gives you the choice of a girl or a boy elephant. The differences between the two are their colors (brown for a boy and pink for a girl), and their accessories (flower for a girl and man-purse for a boy).

yarn

1 skein Cascade Yarns 220 Superwash (100% wool, 220 yds ea) in color #836 Pink (MC) for girl elephant

1 skein Cascade Yarns 220 Superwash (100% wool, 220 yds ea) in color #819 Brown (MC) for boy elephant

1 skein Cascade Yarns 220 Superwash (100% wool, 220 yds ea) in color #824 Yellow (CC1) for both

1 skein Dale of Norway Dale Baby Ull (100% wool, 192 yds ea) in color #0020 Off White (CC2) for accessories

hooks and notions

size F/5 (3.75mm) hook
size D/3 (3.25mm) hook
If necessary, change hook size to obtain gauge.
100% polyester fiberfill
1 pair 15 mm pink or brown animal eyes (Suzusei)
yellow glitter pom-pom (Darice)
white or pink pre-made foam heart(s) (Darice)
fabric glue
stitch marker
yarn needle

gauge

19 sc x 14 rows = 4" (10cm)

finished size

5½" (14cm) tall

notes

See page 9 for information on working in the round and decreasing.

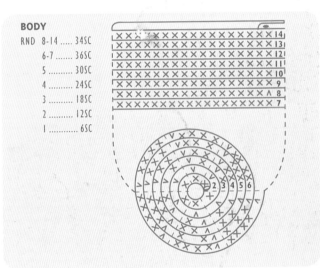

BODY		
RND 8-14	34 SC	
6-7	36 SC	
5	30 SC	
4	24 SC	
3	18 SC	
2	12 SC	
1	6 SC	

BODY

With MC and larger hook, ch 4, sl st in first ch to form ring.

RND 1: Ch 1, 6 sc into ring, place marker in last st to mark end of rnd. Do not join in first st—6 sc total.

RND 2: Work 2 sc in each st around, replace marker in last st throughout pattern—12 sc total.

RND 3: * Sc in next st, 2 sc in next st; rep from * around—18 sc total.

RND 4: * Sc in each of next 2 sts, 2 sc in next st; rep from * around—24 sc total.

RND 5: * Sc in each of next 3 sts, 2 sc in next st; rep from * around—30 sc total.

RND 6: * Sc in each of next 4 sts, 2 sc in next st; rep from * around—36 sc total.

RND 7: Sc in each st around.

RND 8: * Dec, sc in each of next 16 sts; rep from * once—34 sc total.

RNDS 9–14: Rep Rnd 7.

Sl st in next st. Fasten off and weave in ends.

HEAD

With MC and larger hook, ch 4, sl st in first ch to form ring.

RND 1: Ch 1, 6 sc into ring, place marker in last st to mark end of rnd. Do not join in first st—6 sc total.

RND 2: Work 2 sc in each st around, replace marker in last st throughout pattern—12 sc total.

RND 3: * Sc in next st, 2 sc in next st; rep from * around—18 sc total.

RND 4: Sc in next st, 2 sc in next st, * sc in each of next 2 sts, 2 sc in next st; rep from * 4 times, sc in last st—24 sc total.

RND 5: Sc in each of next 2 sts, 2 sc in next st, * sc in each of next 3 sts, 2 sc in next st; rep from * 4 times, sc in last st—30 sc total.

RND 6: Sc in each of next 2 sts, 2 sc in next st, * sc in each of next 4 sts, 2 sc in next st; rep from * 4 times, sc in each of last 2 sts—36 sc total.

RND 7: Sc in each of next 3 sts, 2 sc in next st, * sc in each of next 5 sts, 2 sc in next st; rep from * 4 times, sc in each of last 2 sts—42 sc total.

RND 8: Sc in each of next 3 sts, 2 sc in next st, * sc in each of next 6 sts, 2 sc in next st; rep from * 4 times, sc in each of last 3 sts—48 sc total.

RND 9: Sc in each of next 4 sts, 2 sc in next st, * sc in each of next 7 sts, 2 sc in next st; rep from *4 times, sc in each of last 3 sts—54 sc total.

RND 10: Sc in each of next 4 sts, 2 sc in next st, * sc in each of next 8 sts, 2 sc in next st; rep from * 4 times, sc in each of last 4 sts—60 sc total.

RNDS 11–12: Sc in each st around.

RND 13: Change to smaller hook, sc in each of next 7 sts, dec, * sc in each of next 13 sts, sc 2 tog over next 2 sts; rep from * twice, sc in each of last 6 sts—56 sc total.

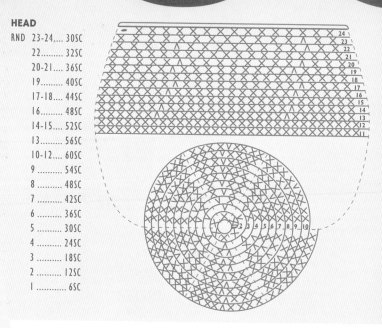

HEAD

RND	SC
23–24	30SC
22	32SC
20–21	36SC
19	40SC
17–18	44SC
16	48SC
14–15	52SC
13	56SC
10–12	60SC
9	54SC
8	48SC
7	42SC
6	36SC
5	30SC
4	24SC
3	18SC
2	12SC
1	6SC

RND 14: Sc in each of next 6 sts, dec, * sc in each of next 12 sts, dec; rep from * twice, sc in each of last 6 sts—52 sc total.

RND 15: Rep Rnd 11.

RND 16: Sc in each of next 5 sts, dec, * sc in each of next 11 sts, dec; rep from * twice, sc in each of last 6 sts—48 sc total.

RND 17: Sc in each of next 4 sts, dec, * sc in each of next 10 sts, dec; rep from * twice, sc in each of last 6 sts—44 sc total.

RND 18: Rep Rnd 11.

RND 19: Sc in each of next 4 sts, dec, * sc in each of next 9 sts, dec; rep from * twice, sc in each of last 6 sts—40 sc total.

RND 20: Sc in each of next 3 sts dec, * sc in each of next 8 sts, dec; rep from * twice, sc in each of last 6 sts—36 sc total.

RND 21: Rep Rnd 11.

RND 22: Sc in each of next 2 sts, dec, * sc in each of next 8 sts, dec; rep from * twice, sc in each of last 2 sts—32 sc total.

RND 23: Sc in each of next 2 sts, dec, * sc in each of next 12 sts, dec; rep from * once—29 sc total.

RND 24: Rep Rnd 11.

Fasten off, leaving a long tail for sewing.

ARMS AND LEGS (make 4)

With CC1 and larger hook, ch 3, sl st in first ch to form ring.

RND 1: Ch 1, 6 sc into ring, place marker in last st to mark end of rnd. Do not join in first st—6 sc total.

RND 2: Work 2 sc in each st around, changing to MC with last st. Replace marker in last st throughout pattern—12 sc total.

RND 3: Sc in each st around.

RND 4: Change to MC, * dec, sc in each of next 4 sts; rep from * once—10 sc total.

RNDS 5–7: Rep Rnd 3.

Sl st in next st. Fasten off, leaving a long tail for sewing.

ARMS & LEGS

RND	
4-7	10SC
2-3	12SC
1	6SC

EARS

With MC and larger hook, ch 3, sl st in first ch to form ring.

RNDS 1–7: Work as for Rnds 1–7 of Body.

Sl st in next st. Fasten off, leaving a long tail for sewing.

TRUNK

With MC and larger hook, ch 3, sl st in first ch to form ring.

RND 1: Ch 1, 6 sc into ring, place marker in last st to mark end of rnd. Do not join in first st—6 sc total.

RND 2: Work 2 sc in each st around. Replace marker in last st throughout pattern—12 sc total.

RNDS 3–4: Sc in each st around.

RND 5: * Dec, sc in each of next 4 sts; rep from * once—10 sc total.

RNDS 6–10: Rep Rnd 3.

Sl st in next st. Fasten off, leaving a long tail for sewing.

TRUNK

RND	
5-10	10SC
2-4	12SC
1	6SC

MAN-PURSE (for Boy Elephant)

With larger hook and CC2, ch 4, sl st in first ch to form ring.

RND 1: Ch 1, 6 sc into ring, place marker in last st to mark end of rnd. Do not join in first st—6 sc total.

RND 2: Work 2 sc in each st around, replace marker in last st throughout pattern—12 sc total.

RNDS 3–5: Sc in each st around.

Sl st in next st. Do not cut the yarn.

STRAP

Ch 32. Fasten off, leaving a long tail. Sew to inside of mini purse on the opposite side.

FLOWER (for Girl Elephant)

With larger hook and CC2, ch 4, sl st in first ch to form ring. Work (ch 3, dc, ch 3, sl st) into ring 5 times—5 petals. Fasten off, leaving a long tail for sewing.

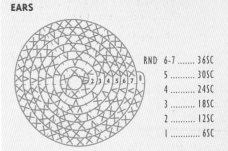

EARS

RND	
6-7	36SC
5	30SC
4	24SC
3	18SC
2	12SC
1	6SC

MAN-PURSE

RND	
2-5	12SC
1	6SC

chain 32

Assembly

Stuff all of the Body parts except the Ears, putting a small amount of stuffing into the Trunk. Then use tail ends and a yarn needle to sew the Ears (folded in half) and Trunk to the Head. Attach the eyes to the Head. Use tail ends to sew the Head, Arms and Legs to the Body. Sew the Flower onto Girl Elephant's head. If desired, accent the center of the Flower with a bead or pom-pom. Weave in any loose ends. See page 109 in the Mr. Funky Wants You to Know section for more information on constructing animals. Glue on a foam heart, if desired.

sebastian *le* hamster

Sebastian *Le* Hamster always wears his fancy beret. Place his eyes on round nine or ten, and place the nose in the vicinity of round twelve. Make sure the nose is precisely between the eyes. And give him an extra helping of stuffing before closing him up.

yarn

1 skein Bernat Cottontots (100% cotton, 171 yds ea) in color #128 Little Boy Blue (MC)

1 skein Bernat Cottontots (100% cotton, 171 yds ea) in color #7 Sweet Cream (CC1)

1 skein Bernat Cottontots (100% cotton, 171 yds ea) in color #615 Sunshine (CC2)

hooks and notions

size F/5 (3.75mm) hook

size D/3 (3.25mm) hook

If necessary, change hook size to obtain gauge.

stitch marker

yarn needle

100% polyester fiberfill

1 pair 15mm new blue plastic crystal eyes (Suzusei)

8mm plastic nose (Darice)

yellow glitter pom-pom (Darice)

gauge

16 sts x 12 rows = 4" (10cm) in sc using larger hook

finished size

7" (18cm) tall, including hat

notes

See page 9 for information on working in the round and decreasing.

BODY

With larger hook and MC, ch 4, sl st in first ch to form ring.

RND 1: Ch 1, 6 sc into ring, place marker in last st to mark end of rnd. Do not join in first st—6 sc total.

RND 2: Work 2 sc in each st around, replace marker in last st throughout pattern—12 sc total.

RND 3: * Sc in next st, 2 sc in next st; rep from * around—18 sc total.

RND 4: * Sc in each of next 2 sts, 2 sc in next st; rep from * around—24 sc total.

RND 5: * Sc in each of next 3 sts, 2 sc in next st; rep from * around—30 sc total.

RND 6: * Sc in each of next 4 sts, 2 sc in next st; rep from * around—36 sc total.

RNDS 7–28: Sc in each st around.

RND 29: Changing to smaller crochet hook, * dec, sc in each of next 4 sts; rep from * around—30 sc total.

RND 30: * Dec, sc in each of next 3 sts; rep from * around—24 sc total.

Begin stuffing the Body, continuing to add stuffing to desired fullness as you complete the Body.

RND 31: * Dec, sc in each of next 2 sts; rep from * around—18 sc total.

RND 32: * Dec, sc in next st; rep from * around—12 sc total.

RND 33: Dec 6 times around—6 sc total.

Sl st in next st. Fasten off, leaving a long tail. Use a yarn needle to weave in ends.

ARMS AND LEGS (make 4)

With larger hook and CC1, ch 3, sl st in first ch to form ring.

RND 1: Ch 1, 5 sc into ring, place marker in last st to mark end of rnd. Do not join in first st—5 sc total.

RND 2: Sc in each st around, replace marker in last st throughout pattern.

RNDS 3–5: Sc in each st around.

Sl st in next st. Fasten off, leaving a long tail for sewing.

BODY

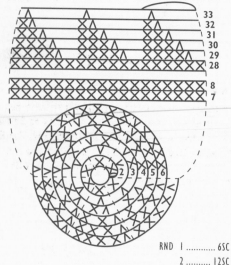

RND	1	6SC
	2	12SC
	3	18SC
	4	24SC
	5	30SC
	6-28	36SC
	29	30SC
	30	24SC
	31	18SC
	32	12SC
	33	6SC

ARMS & LEGS

RND 1-5 .... 5SC

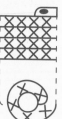

EARS (make 2)

With larger hook and CC1, ch 4, sl st in first ch to form ring.

RND 1: Work 8 sc into ring, place marker in last st to mark end of rnd. Do not join in first st—8 sc total.

RND 2: Sc in each st around, replace marker in last st throughout pattern.

RND 3: Sc in each st around.
Sl st in next st. Fasten off, leaving a long tail for sewing.

AROUND NOSE (make 1)

Work as for Ears.

BERET

With larger hook and CC2, ch 4, sl st in first ch to form ring.

RNDS 1–4: Work as for Rnds 1–4 of Body.

RND 5: Sc in each st around.

RND 6: * Dec, sc in each of next 3 sts; rep from * around, ending sc in each of last 2 sts—19 sc total.
Make sure the Body is firmly stuffed. Sl st in next st. Fasten off, leaving a long tail for sewing.

BERET

RND	
1	6SC
2	12SC
3	18SC
4-5	24SC
6	19SC

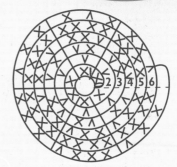

EARS & AROUND NOSE

RND	
1-3	8SC

Assembly

Secure the plastic nose to Around Nose, and secure the plastic eyes to the Body. Use tail ends and a yarn needle to sew the Ears and Around Nose to the Body. Use tail ends to sew Arms, Legs and Beret to the Body. (Ears, Arms and Legs do not require stuffing.) Weave in any loose ends.

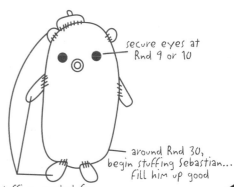

secure eyes at Rnd 9 or 10

around Rnd 30, begin stuffing Sebastian... fill him up good

no stuffing needed for Ears, Arms and Legs

funky spunky **monkey** and pretty little **kitty**

A funky, spunky, not-so-chunky monkey and a pretty little kitty can be made using the same pattern for the body, face, arms, legs and tail. Meow's wire whiskers make her stop going bananas and create absolute purrrfection.

yarn

1 skein Caron Perfect Match (100% acrylic, 355 yds ea) in Sunflower (MC for cat, CC for monkey)

1 skein Red Heart Super Saver (100% acrylic, 364 yds ea) in Aran (MC for monkey, CC for cat)

Plus scraps of yarn in colors of your choice for the scarves.

hooks and notions

size F/5 (3.75mm) hook

size D/3 (3.25mm) hook
If necessary, change hook size to obtain gauge.

100% polyester fiberfill

24" (60cm) fun wire for cat's whiskers

1 pair 12mm yellow plastic cat's eyes for cat (Suzusei)

1 pair 12mm animal eyes for monkey (Suzusei)

8mm plastic nose each for monkey and cat (Darice)

pre-made red and white foam hearts (Darice)

stitch marker

yarn needle

fabric glue

gauge

16 sc x 11 rows = 4" (10cm) using larger hook

finished size

12" (30cm) tall, not including tail or ears

notes

See page 9 for information on working in the round and decreasing.

BODY (for Monkey and Cat)

With larger hook and CC, ch 4, sl st in first ch to form ring.

RND 1: Ch 1, 6 sc into ring, place marker in last st to mark end of rnd. Do not join in first st—6 sc total.

RND 2: Work 2 sc in each st around, replace marker in last st throughout pattern—12 sc total.

RND 3: * Sc in next st, 2 sc in next st; rep from * around—18 sc total.

RND 4: * 2 sc in next st, sc in each of next 2 sts; rep from * around—24 sc total.

RND 5: Sc in next st, 2 sc in next st, * sc in each of next 3 sts, 2 sc in next st; rep from * 4 times, sc in each of last 2 sts—30 sc total.

RNDS 6–7: Sc in each st around.

RND 8: * Sc in each of next 13 sts, dec; rep from * once—28 sc total.

RND 9: Sc in each of next 6 sts, dec, sc in each of next 12 sts, dec, sc in each st to end of rnd—26 sc total.

RND 10: Rep Rnd 6.

RND 11: Dec, sc in each of next 13 sts, dec, sc in each st to end of rnd—24 sc total.

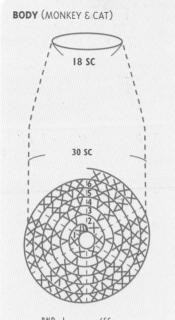

BODY (MONKEY & CAT)

18 SC

30 SC

RND	
1	6SC
2	12SC
3	18SC
4	24SC
5–7	30SC
8	28SC
9–10	26SC
11–12	24SC
13–14	22SC
15–16	20SC
17–18	18SC

RND 12: Rep Rnd 6.

RND 13: Sc in each of next 4 sts, dec, sc in each of next 10 sts, dec, sc in each st to end of rnd—22 sc total.

RND 14: Rep Rnd 6.

RND 15: Dec, sc in each of next 9 sts, dec, sc in each st to end of rnd—20 sc total.

RND 16: Rep Rnd 6.

RND 17: Sc in each of next 2 sts, dec, sc in each of next 8 sts, dec, sc in each st to end of rnd—18 sc total.

RND 18: Rep Rnd 6.

Sl st in next st. Fasten off and weave in ends.

HEAD (for Monkey and Cat)

With larger hook and MC, ch 4, sl st in first ch to form ring.

RNDS 1–5: Work as for Rnds 1–5 of Body.

RND 6: Sc in each of next 3 sts, 2 sc in next, * sc in each of next 4 sts, 2 sc in next st; rep from * 4 times, sc in last st of rnd—36 sc total.

RND 7: * Sc in each of next 5 sts, 2 sc in next; rep from * 5 times—42 sc total.

RND 8: * 2 sc in next st, sc in each of next 6 sts; rep from * 5 times—48 sc total.

RNDS 9–10: Sc in each st around.

RND 11: * Sc in each of next 22 sts, dec; rep from * once—46 sc total.

RND 12: Switch to smaller hook, * sc in each of next 7 sts, dec; rep from * 4 times, ending with sc in last st—41 sc total.

RND 13: Sc in each of next 5 sts, dec, * sc in each of next 6 sts, dec; rep from * 3 times, ending with sc in each of last 2 sts—36 sc total.

RND 14: Sc in each of next 3 sts, dec, * sc in each of next 5 sts, dec; rep 3 times, sc in each of last 3 sts—31 sc total.

RND 15: Sc in next st, dec, * sc in each of next 4 sts, dec; rep from * 3 times, sc in each of last 4 sts—26 sc total.

●	slip stitch
0	chain
✕	single crochet
V	2 single crochet in one
∧	1 single crochet

RND 16: Dec, * sc in each of next 4 sts, dec; rep from * around—21 sc total.

RND 17: Sc in next st, * dec, sc in each of next 2 sts; rep from * around.
Sl st in next st. Fasten off, leaving a long tail for sewing.

LEGS AND ARMS (make 4 each for Monkey and Cat)

With larger hook and CC, ch 4, sl st in first ch to form ring.

RND 1: Ch 1, 6 sc into ring, place marker in last st to mark end of rnd. Do not join in first st—6 sc total.

RND 2: Work 2 sc in each st around, replace marker in last st throughout pattern—12 sc total.

RND 3: Sc in each st around.

RND 4: Switch to smaller hook and MC, * sc in each of next 2 sts, dec; rep from * around—9 sc total.

RNDS 5–21: Switch to larger hook, sc in each st around.

RND 22: Sc in each st around to last st, sl st in last st.
Sl st in next st. Fasten off, leaving a long tail for sewing.

TAIL (for Monkey and Cat)

With larger hook and MC, ch 4, sl st in first ch to form ring.

RND 1: Work 7 sc into ring, place marker in last st to mark end of rnd. Do not join in first st—7 sc total.

RNDS 2–25: Sc in each st around, replace marker in last st throughout pattern.
Sl st in next st. Fasten off, leaving a long tail for sewing.

HEAD (MONKEY & CAT)

RND 1 .... 6SC	RND 8-10 .... 48SC
2 .... 12SC	11 .... 46SC
3 .... 18SC	12 .... 41SC
4 .... 24SC	13 .... 36SC
5 .... 30SC	14 .... 31SC
6 .... 36SC	15 .... 26SC
7 .... 42SC	16 .... 21SC
	17 .... 16SC

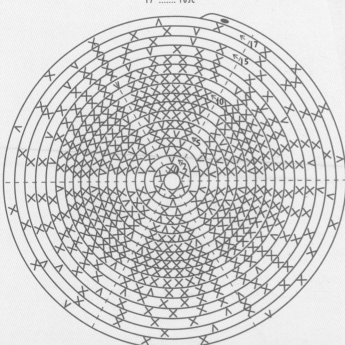

FACE (for Monkey)

With CC, work Rnds 1–6 as for Head.
Sl st in next st. Fasten off, leaving a long tail for sewing.

MONKEY EARS (make 2)

With larger hook and MC, ch 4, sl st in first ch to form ring.

RND 1: Ch 1, 6 sc into ring, place marker in last st to mark end of rnd. Do not join in first st—6 sc total.

RND 2: Work 2 sc in each st around, replace marker in last st throughout pattern—12 sc total.

RNDS 3–4: Sc in each st around.
Sl st in next st. Fasten off, leaving a long tail for sewing.

CAT EARS (make 2)

With larger hook and CC, ch 4, sl st in first ch to form ring.

RND 1: Ch 1, 6 sc into ring, place marker in last st to mark end of rnd. Do not join in first st—6 sc total.

RND 2: Sc in each st around, replace marker in last st throughout pattern—6 sc total.

RND 3: Work 2 sc in each st around—12 sc total.

RND 4: Rep Rnd 2.

RND 5: * Sc in next st, 2 sc in next st; rep from * around—18 sc total.

RNDS 6–7: Rep Rnd 2.
Sl st in next st. Fasten off, leaving a long tail for sewing.

LEGS & ARMS (CAT & MONKEY)

RND	
1	6 SC
2	12 SC
4-22	9 SC

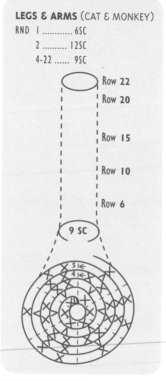

TAIL (CAT & MONKEY)

RNDS 1-25 .... 7 SC

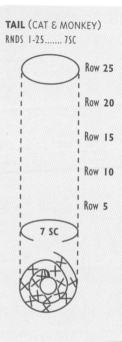

FACE (MONKEY ONLY)

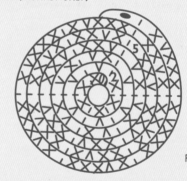

RND	
1	6 SC
2	12 SC
3	18 SC
4	24 SC
5	30 SC
6	36 SC

EARS (MONKEY ONLY)

RND 1 .... 6SC
2-4 .... 12SC

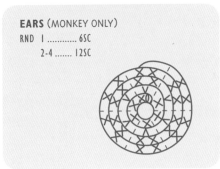

EARS (CAT ONLY)

RND 1-2 .... 26SC
3-4 .... 12SC
5-7 .... 18SC

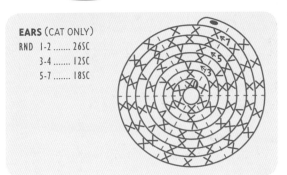

ASSEMBLY

Funky Spunky Monkey

Stuff all of the parts except for the Ears with fiberfill. Secure the plastic eyes and nose to the Face. Use tail ends and a yarn needle to sew the Face and Ears to the Head. Use tail ends to sew the Head, Arms, Legs and Tail to the Body. Weave in any loose ends. Use fabric glue to adhere foam hearts to Monkey's chest, if desired.

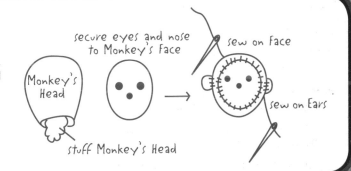

secure eyes and nose to Monkey's Face

sew on face

Monkey's Head

sew on Ears

stuff Monkey's Head

ASSEMBLY

Pretty Little Kitty

Stuff all of the parts except the Ears with fiberfill, as for the Monkey. Secure the plastic eyes to the Head. Follow the construction diagram to secure the whiskers to the Cat's Face. Use tail ends and a yarn needle to sew the Ears to the Head. Use tail ends to sew the Head, Arms, Legs and Tail to the Body. Weave in any loose ends. Use fabric glue to adhere foam hearts to Kitty's chest, if desired.

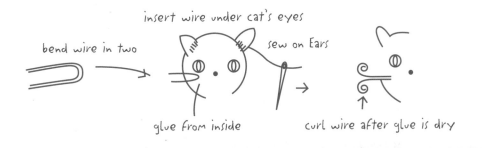

insert wire under cat's eyes

bend wire in two

sew on Ears

glue from inside

curl wire after glue is dry

panda bear
keychains

One of these keychains makes the perfect accessory for your Porsche or Vespa, mansion or houseboat. This is a small yet delicate project that requires patience and attention to detail. Attach the key holder onto the head of the panda bear and keep it snug with the scarf.

yarn

1 skein Bernat Baby (100% acrylic, 286 yds ea) in color #402 White (MC)

1 skein Bernat Baby (100% acrylic, 286 yds ea) in color #451 Baby Blue (boy) or color #469 Pink (girl) (CC1)

scraps of Cascade 220 superwash (100% wool) in color #836 Pink (for girl's scarf) and in color #824 Yellow (for boy's scarf)

hooks and notions

size C/2 (2.75mm) hook

size B/1 (2.25mm) hook

If necessary, change hook size to obtain gauge.

stitch marker

yarn needle

1 pair 4mm google eyes in pink or blue (Suzusei)

4mm nose (Darice)

100% polyester fiberfill

key ring

fabric glue

gauge

20 sc x 22 rows = 4" (10cm) with larger hook

24 sc x 25 rows = 4" (10cm) with smaller hook

finished size

3½" (9cm) tall

notes

See page 9 for information on working in the round and decreasing.

HEAD

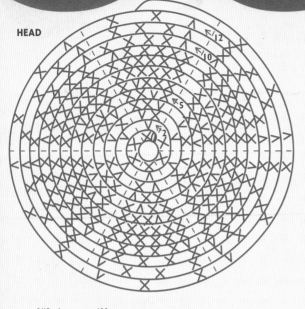

RND	1	6SC		RND	6-7	36SC
	2	12SC			8	34SC
	3	18SC			9	30SC
	4	24SC			10	25SC
	5	30SC			11	20SC
					12	15SC

BODY

RND	1	6SC
	2	12SC
	3	18SC
	4	24SC
	5-6	30SC
	7-9	32SC
	10	30SC
	11	28SC
	12	28SC
	13	26SC
	14	24SC
	15	22SC
	16	20SC

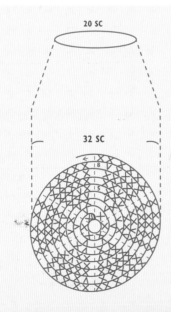

20 SC

32 SC

HEAD

With MC and larger hook, ch 3, sl st in first ch to form ring.

RND 1: Ch 1, 6 sc into ring, place marker in last st to mark end of rnd. Do not join in first st—6 sc total.

RND 2: Work 2 sc in each st around, replace marker in last st throughout pattern—12 sc total.

RND 3: * Sc in next st, 2 sc in next st; rep from * around—18 sc total.

RND 4: * 2 sc in next st, sc in each of next 2 sts; rep from * around—24 sc total.

RND 5: Sc in next st, * 2 sc in next st, sc in each of next 3 sts; rep from * around, ending sc in each of last 2 sts—30 sc total.

RND 6: Sc in each of next 3 sts, *2 sc in next st, sc in each of next 4 sts; rep from * around, ending with sc in last st—36 sc total.

RND 7: Sc in each st around.

RND 8: * Sc in each of next 16 sts, dec; rep from * once—34 sc total.

RND 9: Switch to smaller hook, * sc in each of next 5 sts, dec; rep from * 3 times, sc in each of last 6 sts—30 sc total.

RND 10: * Dec, sc in each of next 4 sts; rep from * around—25 sc total.

RND 11: * Dec, sc in each of next 3 sts; rep from * around—20 sc total.

RND 12: * Dec, sc in each of next 2 st; rep from * around—15 sc total.

Sl st in next st. Fasten off, leaving a long tail for sewing.

BODY

With MC and smaller hook, ch 3, sl st in first ch to form ring.

RNDS 1–5: Work as for Rnds 1–5 of Head.

RND 6: Sc in each st around.

RND 7: * Sc in each of next 14 sts, 2 sc in next st; rep from * once—32 sc total.

RNDS 8–9: Rep Rnd 6.

RND 10: Dec, sc in each of next 10 sts, dec, sc in each st around—30 sc total.

RND 11: Sc in each of next 6 sts, dec, sc in each of next 11 sts, dec, sc in each st around—28 sc total.

RND 12: Rep Rnd 6.

RND 13: Dec, sc in each of next 8 sts, dec, sc in each st around—26 sc total.

RND 14: Sc in each of next 5 sts, dec, sc in each of next 9 sts, dec, sc in each st around—24 sc total.

RND 15: Dec, sc in each of next 6 sts, dec, sc in each st around—22 sc total.

ARMS & LEGS
RND 1-7 .... 6SC

RND 16: Sc in each of next 4 sts, dec, sc in each of next 7 sts, dec, sc in each st around—20 sc total.
Sl st in next st. Fasten off and weave in ends.

ARMS AND LEGS (make 4)

With CC and smaller hook, ch 3, sl st in first ch to form ring.

RND 1: Ch 1, 6 sc into ring, place marker in last st to mark end of rnd. Do not join in first st—6 sc total.

RNDS 2–7: Sc in each st around, replace marker in last st throughout pattern.
Sl st in next st. Fasten off, leaving a long tail for sewing.

EARS (make 2)

With CC and smaller hook, ch 3, sl st in first ch to form ring.

RND 1: Ch 1, 5 sc into ring, place marker in last st to mark end of rnd. Do not join in first st—5 sc total.

RND 2: Work 2 sc in each st around, replace marker in last st throughout pattern—10 sc total.

RNDS 3–4: Sc in each st around.
Sl st in next st. Fasten off, leaving a long tail for sewing.

AROUND EYES (make 2)

With CC and smaller hook, ch 3, sl st in first ch to form ring.

RND 1: Work 6 sc into ring, sl st in first sc to join—6 sc total.
Fasten off, leaving a long tail for sewing.

EARS
RND 1 .... 5SC
2-4 .... 10SC

AROUND EYES
RND 1 .... 6SC

Assembly

Stuff all parts except the Ears with fiberfill, and use tail ends and a yarn needle to sew the Ears and Around Eyes (after eyes are glued on) to the Head. Secure the plastic nose between the eyes. Using tail ends, sew the Head, Arms and Legs to the Body. Weave in any loose ends.

glue eyes on Around Eyes

sew Around Eyes on the face

secure key holder on top of Panda's Head

the real
mr. funky

Let me introduce you to the real Mr. Funky. This pink bear has a lot of heart and would love to snuggle with you anytime, whether you're feeling blue or you're just in the mood to give a little lovin'. Mr. Funky wants to be your best friend.

yarn

1 skein Red Heart Super Saver (100% acrylic, 364 yds ea) in Fuchsia (MC)

1 skein Red Heart Super Saver (100% acrylic, 364 yds ea) in Aran (CC)

light pink scrap yarn for scarf

hooks and notions

size F/5 (3.75mm) hook

size D/3 (3.25mm) hook

If necessary, change hook size to obtain gauge.

100% polyester fiberfill

stitch marker

yarn needle

1 pair 30mm comical eyes (Suzusei)

8mm black nose (Darice)

pre-made red and pink foam hearts (Darice)

fabric glue

gauge

16 sc x 11 rows = 4" (10cm) with larger hook

finished size

10" (25cm) tall

notes

See page 9 for information on working in the round and decreasing.

HEAD

With larger hook and MC, ch 4, sl st in first ch to form ring.

RND 1: Ch 1, 7 sc into ring, place marker in last st to mark end of rnd. Do not join in first st—7 sc total.

RND 2: Work 2 sc in each st around, replace marker in last st throughout pattern—14 sc total.

RND 3: * Sc in next st, 2 sc in next st; rep from * around—21 sc total.

RND 4: * 2 sc in next st, sc in each of next 2 sts; rep from * around—28 sc total.

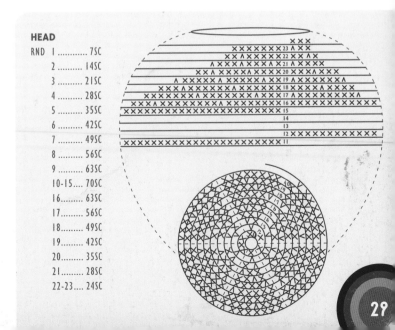

HEAD	
RND 1	7 SC
2	14 SC
3	21 SC
4	28 SC
5	35 SC
6	42 SC
7	49 SC
8	56 SC
9	63 SC
10-15	70 SC
16	63 SC
17	56 SC
18	49 SC
19	42 SC
20	35 SC
21	28 SC
22-23	24 SC

RND 5: Sc in each of next 2 sts, 2 sc in next st, * sc in each of next 3 sts, 2 sc in next st; rep from * around, ending with sc in last st—35 sc total.

RND 6: * Sc in each of next 4 sts, 2 sc in next st; rep from * around—42 sc total.

RND 7: * 2 sc in next st, sc in each of next 5 sts; rep from * around—49 sc total.

RND 8: Sc in each of next 2 sts, 2 sc in next st, * sc in each of next 6 sts, 2 sc in next st; rep from * around, ending sc in each of last 4 sts—56 sc total.

RND 9: Sc in each of next 4 sts, 2 sc in next, * sc in each of next 7 sts, 2 sc in next st; rep from * around, ending with sc in each of last 3 sts—63 sc total.

RND 10: Sc in each of next 6 sts, 2 sc in next, * sc in each of next 8 sts, 2 sc in next st; rep from * around, ending sc in each of last 2 sts—70 sc total.

RNDS 11–15: Sc in each st around.

RND 16: Switch to smaller hook, * sc in each of next 8 sts, dec; rep from * around—63 sc total.

RND 17: Sc in each of next 3 sts, dec, * sc in each of next 7 sts, dec; rep from * around, ending sc in last 4 sts—56 sc total.

RND 18: * Sc in each of next 6 sts, dec; rep from * around—49 sc total.

RND 19: Sc in each of next 2 sts, dec, * sc in each of next 5 sts, dec; rep from * around, ending sc in each of last 3 sts—42 sc total.

RND 20: * Sc in each of next 4 sts, dec; rep from * around—35 sc total.

RND 21: Sc in next st, dec, * sc in each of next 3 sts, dec; rep from * around, sc in each of last 2 sts—28 sc total.

RND 22: * Sc in each of next 5 sts, dec; rep from * around—24 sc total.

RND 23: Sc in each st around.

Sl st in next st. Fasten off, leaving a long tail for sewing.

BODY

With larger hook and CC, ch 4, sl st in first ch to form ring.

RNDS 1–6: Work as for Rnds 1–6 of Head.

RNDS 7–11: Sc in each st around.

RND 12: * Sc in each of next 4 sts, dec; rep from * around—35 sc total.

RNDS 13–18: Rep Rnd 7.

RND 19: * Dec, sc in each of next 3 sts; rep from * around—28 sc total.

RNDS 20–24: Rep Rnd 7.

RND 25: * Sc in each of next 5 sts, dec; rep from * around—24 sc total.

Sl st in next st. Fasten off and weave in ends.

BODY

RND	
1	7SC
2	14SC
3	21SC
4	28SC
5	35SC
6-11	42SC
12-18	35SC
19-24	28SC
25	24SC

EARS

RND	
1	6SC
2	12SC
3-5	18SC

EARS (make 2)

With larger hook and CC, ch 4, sl st in first ch to form ring.

RND 1: Ch 1, 6 sc into ring, place marker in last st to mark end of rnd. Do not join in first st—6 sc total.

RND 2: Work 2 sc in each st around, replace marker in last st throughout pattern—12 sc total.

RND 3: * Sc in next st, 2 sc in next st; rep from * around—18 sc total.

RNDS 4–5: Sc in each st around.
Sl st in next st. Fasten off, leaving a long tail for sewing.

AROUND NOSE

With larger hook and CC, ch 4, sl st in first ch to form ring.

RND 1: Ch 1, 7 sc into ring, place marker in last st to mark end of rnd. Do not join in first st—7 sc total.

RND 2: Work 2 sc in each st around, replace marker in last st throughout pattern—14 sc total.

RND 3: * Sc in next st, 2 sc in next st; rep from * around—21 sc total.
Sl st in next st. Fasten off, leaving a long tail for sewing.
Attach plastic nose to the Around Nose section.

LEGS (make 2)

With larger hook and CC, ch 4, sl st in first ch to form ring.

RND 1: Ch 1, 8 sc into ring, place marker in last st to mark end of rnd. Do not join in first st—8 sc total.

RND 2: Work 2 sc in each st around, replace marker in last st throughout pattern—16 sc total.

RND 3: Sc in each st around.

RNDS 4–6: Switch to MC, sc in each st around.

RND 7: Dec, sc in each st around—15 sc total.

RNDS 8–10: Sc in each st around.

RND 11: Rep Rnd 7—14 sc total.

RND 12: Rep Rnd 8.
Sl st in next st. Fasten off, leaving a long tail for sewing.

ARMS (make 2)

With larger hook and CC, ch 4, sl st in first ch to form ring.

RND 1: Ch 1, 5 sc into ring, place marker in last st to mark end of rnd. Do not join in first st—5 sc total.

RND 2: Work 2 sc in each st around, replace marker in last st throughout pattern—10 sc total.

RND 3: Sc in each st around.

RNDS 4–12: Switch to MC, sc in each st around.

RND 13: Dec, sc in each st around—9 sc total.

RNDS 14–15: Rep Rnd 4.
Sl st in next st. Fasten off, leaving a long tail for sewing.

AROUND NOSE

RND	
1	7SC
2	14SC
3	21SC

LEGS

RND	
1	8SC
2-6	16SC
7-10	15SC
11-12	14SC

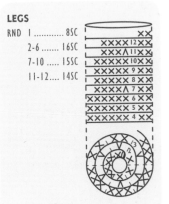

ARMS

RND	
1	5SC
2-12	10SC
13-15	9SC

Assembly

Stuff the Head with fiberfill. Then secure the plastic eyes to the Head. Use tail ends and a yarn needle to sew the Ears and Around Nose to the Head. Use tail ends to sew the Head, Arms and Legs to the Body. Weave in any loose ends. If desired, adhere foam hearts to Mr. Funky with fabric glue.

curve the Ears a little when sewing to Head

sew on Around Nose... no stuffing needed

a hare and a bear

This pattern is a good example of how you can make different animals with just a few modifications. The body, face, arms and legs of the Hare and the Bear (pictured on page 37) are the same except for the ears and around the nose. Symmetry is important to ensure this Hare and Bear look just right.

yarn

1 skein Red Heart Super Saver (100% acrylic, 364 yds ea) in Spruce (MC for Hare, CC for Bear)

1 skein Red Heart Super Saver (100% acrylic, 364 yds ea) in Aran (CC for Hare, MC for Bear)

scrap of Bernat Cottontots (100% cotton) in Sunshine for Hare's Scarf

scrap of Lion Brand Landscapes (wool/acrylic blend) in Summer Fields for Bear's Scarf

hooks and notions

size F/5 (3.75mm) hook

size D/3 (3.25mm) hook
If necessary, change hook size to obtain gauge.

stitch marker

yarn needle

100% polyester fiberfill

8mm plastic nose (Darice)

1 pair 12mm moss green animal eyes for Bear (Suzusei)

1 pair 12mm animal eyes for Hare

pre-made red foam heart(s) (Darice)

fabric glue

gauge

16 sc x 11 rows = 4" (10cm) with larger hook

finished size

10¾" (27cm) tall (not including ears)

notes

See page 9 for information on working in the round and decreasing.

BODY (for Hare and Bear)

With larger hook and CC, ch 4, sl st in first ch to form ring.

RND 1: Ch 1, 6 sc into ring, place marker in last st to mark end of rnd. Do not join in first st—6 sc total.

RND 2: Work 2 sc in each st around, replace marker in last st throughout pattern—12 sc total.

RND 3: * Sc in next st, 2 sc in next st; rep from * around—18 sc total.

RND 4: * 2 sc in next st, sc in each of next 2 sts; rep from * around—24 sc total.

RND 5: Sc in next st, 2 sc in next st, * sc in each of next 3 sts, 2 sc in next st; rep from * 4 times, sc in each of last 2 sts—30 sc total.

RNDS 6–7: Sc in each st around.

RND 8: * Sc in each of next 13 sts, dec; rep from * once—28 sc total.

RND 9: Sc in each of next 6 sts, dec, sc in each of next 12 sts, dec, sc in each st to end of rnd—26 sc total.

RNDS 10–11: Rep Rnd 6.

RND 12: Dec, sc in each of next 13 sts, dec, sc in each st to end of rnd—24 sc total.

RND 13: Sc in each of next 4 sts, dec, sc in each of next 10 sts, dec, sc in each st to end of rnd—22 sc total.

RND 14: Rep Rnd 6.

RND 15: Dec, sc in each of next 9 sts, dec, sc in each st to end of rnd—20 sc total.

RND 16: Sc in each of next 2 sts, dec, sc in each of next 8 sts, dec, sc in each st to end of rnd—18 sc total.

RND 17: Rep Rnd 6.

Sl st in next st. Fasten off and weave in ends.

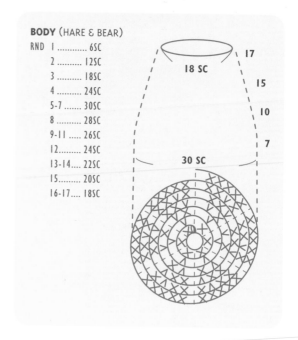

BODY (HARE & BEAR)

RND	
1	6 SC
2	12 SC
3	18 SC
4	24 SC
5-7	30 SC
8	28 SC
9-11	26 SC
12	24 SC
13-14	22 SC
15	20 SC
16-17	18 SC

18 SC · 17 · 15 · 10 · 7 · 30 SC

✗ Single Crochet

∧ Decreasing 2 SC in 1 SC

∨ Increasing 1 SC to 2 SC

● Slip Stitch

ARMS & LEGS (HARE & BEAR)

RND 1 .... 6SC
2 .... 12SC
3-22 .... 9SC

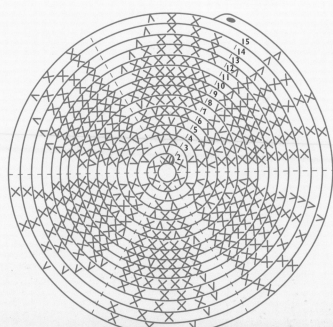

HEAD (for Hare and Bear)

With larger hook and MC, ch 4, sl st in first ch to form ring.

RNDS 1–5: Work as for Rnds 1–5 of Body.

RND 6: Sc in each of next 3 sts, 2 sc in next, * sc in each of next 4 sts, 2 sc in next st; rep from * 4 times, sc in last st of rnd—36 sc total.

RND 7: * Sc in each of next 5 sts, 2 sc in next; rep from * 5 times—42 sc total.

RNDS 8–9: Sc in each st around.

RND 10: * Sc in each of next 19 sts, dec; rep from *once—40 sc total.

RND 11: Switch to smaller hook,*sc in each of next 6 sts, dec; rep from * around—35 sc total.

RND 12: * Sc in each of next 5 sts, dec; rep from * around—30 sc total.

RND 13: * Sc in each of next 4 sts, dec; rep from * around—25 sc total.

RND 14: * Sc in each of next 3 sts, dec; rep from * around—20 sc total.

RND 15: * Sc in each of next 2 sts, dec; rep from * around—14 sc total.

Sl st in next st. Fasten off, leaving a long tail for sewing.

HEAD (HARE & BEAR)

RND		RND		RND	
1 .... 6SC		5 .... 30SC		11 .... 35SC	
2 .... 12SC		6 .... 36SC		12 .... 30SC	
3 .... 18SC		7-9 .... 42SC		13 .... 25SC	
4 .... 24SC		10 .... 40SC		14 .... 20SC	
				15 .... 15SC	

LEGS AND ARMS (make 4 each for Hare and Bear)

With larger hook and CC, ch 4, sl st in first ch to form ring.

RND 1: Ch 1, 6 sc into ring, place marker in last st to mark end of rnd. Do not join in first st—6 sc total.

RND 2: Work 2 sc in each st around, replace marker in last st throughout pattern—12 sc total.

RND 3: Switch to smaller hook, *sc in each of next 2 sts, dec; rep from * around—9 sc total.

RND 4: Switch to larger hook and MC, sc in each st around.

RNDS 5–22: Sc in each st around.

Sl st in next st. Fasten off, leaving a long tail for sewing.

EARS (make 2 for Bear)

With larger hook and CC, ch 4, sl st in first ch to form ring.

RND 1: Ch 1, 6 sc into ring, place marker in last st to mark end of rnd. Do not join in first st—6 sc total.

RND 2: Work 2 sc in each st around, replace marker in last st throughout pattern—12 sc total.

RNDS 3—4: Sc in each st around.

Sl st in next st. Fasten off, leaving a long tail for sewing.

AROUND NOSE (for Bear)

With larger hook and CC, ch 4, sl st in first ch to form ring.

RND 1: Ch 1, 6 sc into ring, place marker in last st to mark end of rnd. Do not join in first st—6 sc total.

RND 2: Work 2 sc in each st around, replace marker in last st throughout pattern—12 sc total.

Sl st in next st. Fasten off, leaving a long tail for sewing. Secure plastic nose to Around Nose.

EARS (make 2 for Hare)

With larger hook and MC, ch 4, sl st in first ch to form ring.

RND 1: Work 8 sc into ring, place marker in last st to mark end of rnd. Do not join in first st—8 sc total.

RNDS 2—12: Sc in each st around, replace marker in last st throughout pattern.

Sl st in next st. Fasten off, leaving a long tail for sewing.

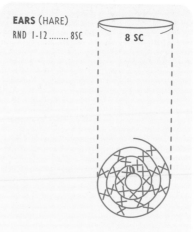

EARS (HARE)
RND 1-12 .... 8SC

8 SC

AROUND NOSE (BEAR)
RND 1 .... 6SC
2 .... 12SC

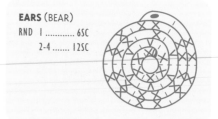

EARS (BEAR)
RND 1 .... 6SC
2-4 .... 12SC

ASSEMBLY

Stuff all the parts except the Ears and Around Nose with fiberfill. Secure the eyes and nose to the Head. Use tail ends and a yarn needle to sew the Ears and Around Nose to the Head. Use tail ends to sew the Head, Arms and Legs to the Body. Weave in any loose ends. See page 109 in the Mr. Funky Wants You to Know section for more instructions on putting your animals together. Glue on a red foam heart to the Hare or the Bear, if desired.

bunny
in a dress

This bunny is a little lady in her sweet dress. The spherical crochet technique for the Amigurumi makes the design look seamless and nearly machine-made. I suggest using a smaller crochet hook when decreasing the stitches to help her keep her stuffing.

yarn

1 skein Lion Brand Jiffy (100% acrylic, 135 yds ea) in color #101 Pastel Pink (MC)

1 skein Lion Brand Wool-Ease (acrylic/wool/rayon blend, 197 yds ea) in color #501 White Frost (CC1)

1 skein Bernat Softee Baby (100% acrylic, 455 yds ea) in color #205 Prettiest Pink (CC2)

hooks and notions

size F/5 (3.75mm) hook

size D/3 (3.25mm) hook

If necessary, change hook size to obtain gauge.

stitch marker

yarn needle

100% polyester fiberfill

1 pair 15mm red/pink crystal plastic eyes (Suzusei)

8mm plastic nose (Darice)

2 buttons

gauge

15 sc x 11 rows = 4" (10cm) with larger hook

finished size

8" (20cm) tall, not including ears

notes

See page 9 for information on working in the round and decreasing.

HEAD

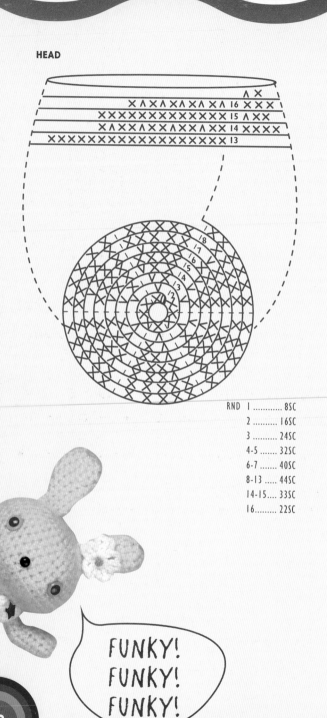

RND	1	8SC
	2	16SC
	3	24SC
	4-5	32SC
	6-7	40SC
	8-13	44SC
	14-15	33SC
	16	22SC

FUNKY!
FUNKY!
FUNKY!

HEAD

With MC and larger hook, ch 4, sl st in first ch to form ring.

RND 1: Ch 1, 8 sc into ring, place marker in last st to mark end of rnd. Do not join in first st—8 sc total.

RND 2: Work 2 sc in each st around, replace marker in last st throughout pattern—16 sc total.

RND 3: * Sc in next st, 2 sc in next st; rep from * around—24 sc total.

RND 4: * Sc in each of next 2 sts, 2 sc in next st; rep from * around—32 sc total.

RND 5: Sc in each st around.

RND 6: * Sc in each of next 3 sts, 2 sc in next st; rep from * around—40 sc total.

RND 7: Rep Rnd 5.

RND 8: * Sc in each of next 4 sts, 2 sc in next st, sc in each of next 5 sts; rep from * around—44 sc total.

RNDS 9–13: Rep Rnd 5.

RND 14: Switch to smaller hook, * sc in each of next 2 sts, dec; rep from * around—33 sc total.

RND 15: Rep Rnd 5.

RND 16: * Sc in next st, dec; rep from * around—22 sc total.

Sl st in next st. Fasten off, leaving a long tail for sewing.

BODY

With MC and larger hook, ch 4, sl st in first ch to form ring.

RND 1: Ch 1, 7 sc into ring, place marker in last st to mark end of rnd. Do not join in first st—7 sc total.

RND 2: Work 2 sc in each st around, replace marker in last st throughout pattern—14 sc total.

RND 3: * Sc in next st, 2 sc in next st; rep from * around—21 sc total.

RND 4: * Sc in each of next 6 sts, 2 sc in next st; rep from * around—24 sc total.

RNDS 5–11: Sc in each st around.

RND 12: Sc in each of next 5 sts, dec, sc in each of next 10 sts, dec, sc in each st to end of rnd—22 sc total.

RND 13: Dec, sc in each of next 9 sts, dec, sc in each st to end of rnd—20 sc total.

RND 14: Rep Rnd 5.

RND 15: Sc in each of next 2 sts, dec, * sc in each of next 5 sts, dec; rep from * once, sc in each of last 2 sts—17 sc total.
Sl st in next st. Fasten off and weave in ends.

EARS (make 2)
With MC and larger hook, ch 4, sl st in first ch to form ring.

RND 1: Ch 1, 6 sc into ring, place marker in last st to mark end of rnd. Do not join in first st—6 sc total.

EARS	
RND 1	6SC
2-4	12SC
5	11SC
6	10SC
7-10	9SC

RND 2: Work 2 sc in each st around, replace marker in last st throughout pattern—12 sc total.

RNDS 3–4: Sc in each st around.

RND 5: Dec, sc in each st around—11 sc total.

RND 6: Sc in each of next 3 sts, dec, sc in each st around—10 sc total.

RND 7: Sc in each of next 6 sts, dec, sc in each of last 2 sts—9 sc total.

RNDS 8–10: Rep Rnd 3.
Sl st in next st. Fasten off, leaving a long tail for sewing.

BODY	
RND 1	7SC
2	14SC
3	21SC
4-11	24SC
12	22SC
13-14	20SC
15	17SC

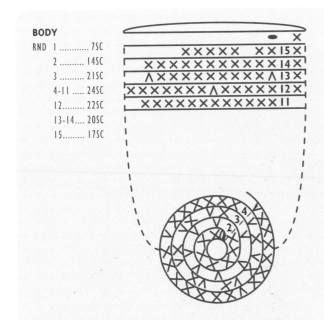

ARMS (make 2)

With MC and larger hook, ch 4, sl st in first ch to form ring.

RND 1: Ch 1, 5 sc into ring, place marker in last st to mark end of rnd. Do not join in first st—5 sc total.

RND 2: Work 2 sc in each st around, replace marker in last st throughout pattern—10 sc total.

RNDS 3–5: Sc in each st around.

RND 6: Sc in each of next 2 sts, dec, sc in each of next 6 sts—9 sc total.

RNDS 7–11: Rep Rnd 3.
Sl st in next st. Fasten off, leaving a long tail for sewing.

LEGS (make 2)

With MC and larger hook, ch 4, sl st in first ch to form ring.

RND 1: Ch 1, 6 sc into ring, place marker in last st to mark end of rnd. Do not join in first st—6 sc total.

RND 2: Work 2 sc in each of next 3 sts, sc in next st, 2 sc in each of next 2 sts, replace marker in last st throughout pattern—11 sc total.

RNDS 3–5: Sc in each st around.

RND 6: Dec, sc in each st around—10 sc total.

RND 7: Sc in each of next 4 sts, dec, sc in each of next 4 sts—9 sc total.

RNDS 8–9: Rep Rnd 3.
Sl st in next st. Fasten off, leaving a long tail for sewing.

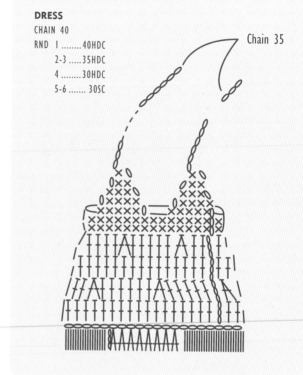

DRESS
CHAIN 40
RND 1 ....40HDC
2-3 .....35HDC
4 ....30HDC
5-6 ....30SC

Chain 35

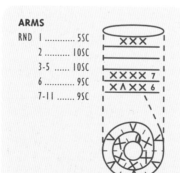

ARMS
RND 1 ....5SC
2 ....10SC
3-5 ......10SC
6 ....9SC
7-11 ......9SC

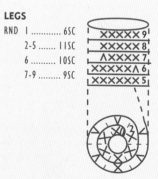

LEGS
RND 1 ....6SC
2-5 ....11SC
6 ....10SC
7-9 ....9SC

DRESS

With smaller hook and CC1, ch 40. Taking care not to twist chain, sl st in first ch to form ring.

RND 1: Ch 2 (counts as hdc), hdc in each st around, sl st in 3rd ch of beg ch-3 to join—40 hdc total.

RND 2: Ch 2 (counts as hdc), hdc in each of next 5 sts, dec, * hdc in each of next 6 sts, dec; rep from * around, sl st in 3rd ch of beg ch-3 to join—35 hdc total.

RND 3: Ch 3 (counts as hdc), hdc in each st around, sl st in 3rd ch of beg ch-3 to join.

RND 4: Ch 3 (counts as hdc), dc in each of next 2 sts, dec, * hdc in each of next 5 sts, dec; rep from * around, ending hdc in each of last 2 sts, sl st in 3rd ch of beg ch-3 to join—30 hdc total.

RNDS 5–6: Ch 1, sc in each st around, sl st in first sc to join.

Front Left Side

ROW 1: Ch 1, sc in first st and in each of next 4 sts, turn—5 sc total.

ROW 2: Ch 1, sc in each of first 4 sts, turn—4 sc total.

ROW 3: Ch 1, sc in each of first 3 sts, turn—3 sc total.

ROW 4: Ch 1, sc in each of first 2 sts, turn—2 sc total.

ROW 5: Ch 1, sc in first st, sl st in next st.
Ch 35 to make tie. Fasten off.

Front Right Side

Skip 3 sts from the last st on Row 1 of Front Left Side, attach yarn in next st. Work as for Front Left Side.

Hem

Working along bottom edge of dress, attach CC2 in any st.

ROW 1: Ch 3 (counts as dc), dc in same st, 2 dc in next st, 3 dc in next st, * 2 dc in each of next 2 sts, 3 dc in next st; rep from * around, sl st in 3rd ch of beg ch-3 to join.
Fasten off and weave in ends.

don't stuff Bunny's Ears, please

stuff Arms & Legs just a bit

tie string at back of Bunny's neck

sew on buttons to front of Dress

Assembly

Stuff all the parts except the Ears with fiberfill, using only a small amount of stuffing for the Arms and Legs. Secure the eyes and nose to the Head. Use tail ends and a yarn needle to sew Ears to the Head. Use tail ends to sew the Head, Arms and Legs to the Body. Sew buttons to the Front Left and Front Right Sides of the Dress. Weave in any loose ends, and dress your bunny.

snazzy stripes snake

This snake pattern is designed with sharp eyes and snazzy stripes. My favorite part is that you get to use turkey loop stitches on the mouth and French knots for the nose. You can wear him as a scarf during Halloween or whenever you want to keep the rats at bay.

yarn

1 skein Bernat Berella 4 (100% acrylic, 195 yds ea) in color #8722 Country Blue (MC)

1 skein Bernat Berella 4 (100% acrylic, 195 yds ea) in color #8720 Light Country Blue (CC)

scrap of Bernat Berella 4 (100% acrylic) in color #8929 Geranium (for Mouth)

hooks and notions

size F/5 (3.75mm) hook
If necessary, change hook size to obtain gauge.

100% polyester fiberfill

1 pair 12mm blue cat eyes (Suzusei)

stitch marker

yarn needle

gauge

16 sc x 8½ rows = 4" (10cm)

finished size

43" (110cm) long

notes

See page 9 for information on working in the round and decreasing.

HEAD

With MC, ch 3, sl st in first ch to form ring.

RND 1: Work 6 sc into ring, place marker in last st to mark end of rnd. Do not join in first st—6 sc total.

RND 2: Work 2 sc in each st around, replace marker in last st throughout pattern—12 sc total.

RND 3: * Sc in next st, 2 sc in next st; rep from * around—18 sc total.

RND 4: Sc in each st around.

RND 5: * 2 sc in next st, sc in each of next 2 sts; rep from * around—24 sc total.

RND 6: Sc in next st, 2 sc in next st, * sc in each of next 3 sts, 2 sc in next st; rep from * 4 times, sc in last st of rnd—30 sc total.

RND 7: Rep Rnd 4.

RND 8: * 2 sc in next st, sc in each of next 4 sts; rep from * around—36 sc total.

RND 9: Sc in each of next 3 sts, 2 sc in next st, * sc in each of next 3 sts, 2 sc in next st; rep from * 4 times, sc in last st of rnd—42 sc total.

RND 10: Rep Rnd 4.

RND 11: * Sc in each of next 6 sts, 2 sc in next st; rep from * around—48 sc total.

RND 12: Sc in each of next 2 sts, 2 sc in next st, * sc in each of next 7 sts, 2 sc in next st; rep from * 4 times, sc in last st of rnd—54 sc total.

HEAD

RND	
1	6SC
2	12SC
3-4	18SC
5	24SC
6-7	30SC
8	36SC
9-10	42SC
11	48SC
12-20	54SC
21-22	48SC
23-31	42SC

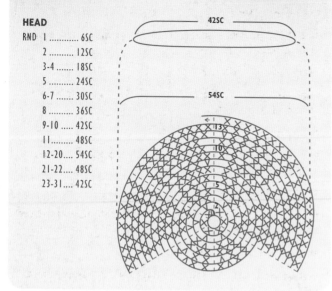

42SC

54SC

RNDS 13–20: Rep Rnd 4.

RND 21: * Sc in each of next 7 sts, dec; rep from * around—48 sc total.

RND 22: Rep Rnd 4.

RND 23: * Sc in each of next 5 sts, dec; rep from * around, ending sc in each of last 6 sts—42 sc total.

RNDS 24–31: Rep Rnd 4.
Fasten off, leaving a long tail for sewing.

BODY

The Body is worked in stripes alternating seven rows of MC with seven rows of CC, ending with five MC rows.
With MC, ch 3, sl st in first ch to form ring.

RND 1: Work 4 sc into ring, place marker in last st to mark end of rnd. Do not join in first st—4 sc total.

RND 2: Work 2 sc in each st around, replace marker in last st throughout pattern—8 sc total.

RND 3: Sc in each st around.

RNDS 4–7: Rep Rnd 3.

RND 8: Work 2 sc in next st, sc in each st around—9 sc total.

RNDS 9–12: Rep Rnd 3.

RND 13: Sc in each of next 2 sts, 2 sc in next st, sc in each st around—10 sc total.

RNDS 14–17: Rep Rnd 3.

RND 18: Sc in each of next 4 sts, 2 sc in next st, sc in each st around—11 sc total.

RNDS 19–22: Rep Rnd 3.

RND 23: Sc in each of next 6 sts, 2 sc in next st, sc in each st around—12 sc total.

RNDS 24–27: Rep Rnd 3.

RND 28: Sc in each of next 8 sts, 2 sc in next st, sc in each st around—13 sc total.

RNDS 29–32: Rep Rnd 3.

RND 33: Sc in each of next 10 sts, 2 sc in next st, sc in each st around—14 sc total.

RNDS 34–37: Rep Rnd 3.

BODY

RND		RND		RND	
1	4SC	98-102	27SC	125	32SC
2-7	8SC	103-107	28SC	126-173	32SC
8-12	9SC	108-112	29SC		
13-17	10SC	113-118	30SC		
18-22	11SC	119-124	31SC		
23-27	12SC				
28-32	13SC				
33-37	14SC				
38-42	15SC				
43-47	16SC				
48-52	17SC				
53-57	18SC				
58-62	19SC				
63-67	20SC				
68-72	21SC				
73-77	22SC				
78-82	23SC				
83-87	24SC				
88-92	25SC				
93-97	26SC				

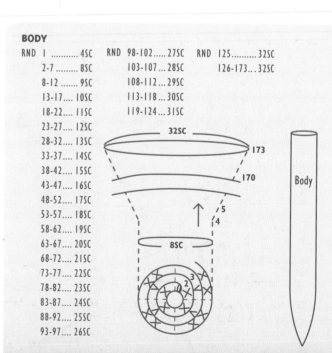

32SC

8SC

Body

RND 38: Sc in each of next 12 sts, 2 sc in next st, sc in each st around—15 sc total.

RNDS 39–42: Rep Rnd 3.

RND 43: Sc in each of next 14 sts, 2 sc in next st, sc in each st around—16 sc total.

RNDS 44–47: Rep Rnd 3.

RND 48: Sc in next st, 2 sc in next st, sc in each st around—17 sc total.

RNDS 49–52: Rep Rnd 3.

RND 53: Sc in each of next 3 sts, 2 sc in next st, sc in each st around—18 sc total.

RNDS 54–57: Rep Rnd 3.

RND 58: Sc in each of next 5 sts, 2 sc in next st, sc in each st around—19 sc total.

RNDS 59–62: Rep Rnd 3.

RND 63: Sc in each of next 7 sts, 2 sc in next st, sc in each st around—20 sc total.

RNDS 64–67: Rep Rnd 3.

RND 68: Sc in each of next 9 sts, 2 sc in next st, sc in each st around—21 sc total.

RNDS 69–72: Rep Rnd 3.

RND 73: Sc in each of next 11 sts, 2 sc in next st, sc in each st around—22 sc total.

RNDS 74–77: Rep Rnd 3.

RND 78: Sc in each of next 13 sts, 2 sc in next st, sc in each st around—23 sc total.

RNDS 79–82: Rep Rnd 3.

RND 83: Sc in each of next 15 sts, 2 sc in next st, sc in each st around—24 sc total.

RNDS 84–87: Rep Rnd 3.

RND 88: Sc in each of next 17 sts, 2 sc in next st, sc in each st around—25 sc total.

RNDS 89–92: Rep Rnd 3.

RND 93: Sc in each of next 19 sts, 2 sc in next st, sc in each st around—26 sc total.

RNDS 94–97: Rep Rnd 3.

RND 98: Sc in each of next 21 sts, 2 sc in next st, sc in each st around—27 sc total.

RNDS 99–102: Rep Rnd 3.

RND 103: Sc in each of next 23 sts, 2 sc in next st, sc in each st around—28 sc total.

RNDS 104–107: Rep Rnd 3.

RND 108: Sc in each of next 25 sts, 2 sc in next st, sc in each st around—29 sc total.

RNDS 109–112: Rep Rnd 3.

RND 113: Sc in each of next 27 sts, 2 sc in next st, sc in each st around—30 sc total.

RNDS 114–118: Rep Rnd 3.

RND 119: Sc in each st around to last 2 sts, 2 sc in next st, sc in last st—31 sc total.

RNDS 120–124: Rep Rnd 3.

RND 125: Rep Rnd 8—32 sc total.

RNDS 126–173: Rep Rnd 3.
Fasten off, leaving a long tail for sewing.

ASSEMBLY

Secure the eyes to the Head. Make two French knots on the Head with a scrap of CC for the nose. Stitch a line of turkey loop stitches with Geranium yarn and a yarn needle to make the mouth. Stuff the Head with polyester fiberfill. Thread a yarn needle onto a long tail end, and sew the Head to the Body. Weave in any loose ends.

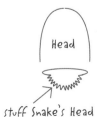

Head

Stuff Snake's Head

BACK VIEW

on-the-go
water bottle carrier

Accessorize your water bottle with this cute bear. This carrier is great for when you're on-the-go with *l'eau* and don't want the chilly condensation sogging you up. I like google eyes, but you can use buttons or felt for eyes and make this bear happy at the gym, picnic, local fairgrounds or even riding the metro.

yarn

1 skein Lily Sugar 'N Cream (100% cotton, 120 yds ea) in color #1742 Hot Blue (MC)

1 skein Bernat Cottontots (100% cotton, 171 yds ea) in color #7 Sweet Cream (CC)

hooks and notions

size F/5 (3.75mm) hook

If necessary, change hook size to obtain gauge.

stitch marker

yarn needle

2 buttons

1 pair 15mm black moving eyes (Suzusei)

15mm black triangular plastic nose

gauge

17 sc x 10 rows = 4" (10cm)

finished size

7½" (19cm) tall, not including strap

notes

See page 9 for information on working in the round and decreasing.

BODY

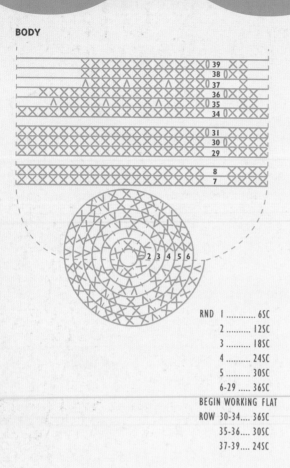

RND	1	....	6SC
	2	....	12SC
	3	....	18SC
	4	....	24SC
	5	....	30SC
	6-29	.....	36SC
BEGIN WORKING FLAT			
ROW	30-34	....	36SC
	35-36	....	30SC
	37-39	....	24SC

BODY

With MC, ch 4, sl st in first ch to form ring.

RND 1: Ch 1, 6 sc into ring, place marker in last st to mark end of rnd. Do not join in first st—6 sc total.

RND 2: Work 2 sc in each st around, replace marker in last st throughout pattern—12 sc total.

RND 3: * Sc in next st, 2 sc in next st; rep from * around—18 sc total.

RND 4: * Sc in each of next 2 sts, 2 sc in next st; rep from * around—24 sc total.

RND 5: * Sc in each of next 3 sts, 2 sc in next st; rep from * around—30 sc total.

RND 6: * Sc in each of next 4 sts, 2 sc in next st; rep from * around—36 sc total.

RNDS 7–29: Sc in each st around.

Split at Back of Carrier

The following rows form the split at the back of the carrier.

ROWS 30–34: Turn, ch 1, sc in each st around.

ROW 35: Turn, ch 1, * sc in each of next 4 sts, dec; rep from * around—30 sc total.

ROW 36: Turn, ch 1, sc in each st around.

ROW 37: Turn, ch 1, * sc in each of next 3 sts, dec; rep from * around—24 sc total.

ROWS 38–39: Turn, ch 1, sc in each st around.
Fasten off, leaving a long tail.

Buttonhole Band

Working along the row ends on the left side of the split, attach MC in the upper right corner. Ch 1, sc in end of first row, sc in end of each of next 4 rows, ch 5, counting backwards, skip previous 3 sc, sl st in next sc. Work 7 sc into ch-5 sp. Continuing across row ends, work 5 sc evenly across next 4 row ends, ch 5, counting backwards, skip previous 3 sc, sl st in next sc. Work 7 sc into ch-5 sp. Sc in last row end.

Fasten off and weave in ends.

GO! GO! GO!

EARS (make 2)

With CC, ch 4, sl st in first ch to form ring.

RND 1: Ch 1, 8 sc into ring, place marker in last st to mark end of rnd. Do not join in first st—8 sc total.

RND 2: Sc in each st around.

RND 3: Sc in each st around to last st, sl st in last st. Fasten off, leaving a long tail for sewing.

STRAP

With MC, leave a long tail for sewing, then ch 126.

ROW 1: Sc in second ch from hook and in each ch across—125 sc total.

ROW 2: Turn, ch 1, sc in each st across. Fasten off, leaving a long tail for sewing.

AROUND NOSE

With CC, work as for Ears. Secure plastic nose to center of Around Nose.

AROUND NOSE & EARS
RND 1-3 .... 8SC

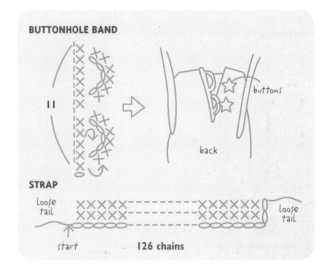

BUTTONHOLE BAND

11

buttons

back

STRAP

loose tail

loose tail

start   126 chains

Assembly

Sew the Strap to the Body securely 1" to 2" (3cm to 5cm) from the top edge of the bag on opposite sides. Use tail ends and a yarn needle to sew the Ears and Nose to the bag. Secure the eyes to the bag as well. Using the button-holes as a guide, sew the buttons onto the right side of the split on the back of the bag. Weave in any loose ends.

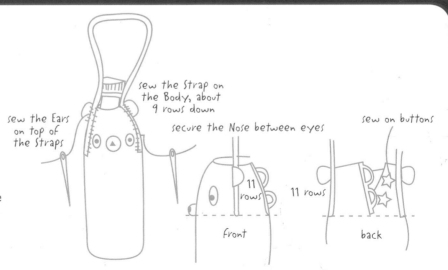

sew the Strap on the Body, about 9 rows down

sew the Ears on top of the Straps

secure the Nose between eyes

sew on buttons

11 rows

11 rows

front

back

MR. FUNKY'S SUPER-

COOL ACCESSORIES

Mr. Funky's
Super-Cool Accessories

This chapter will show you how to make whimsical accessories that accent your favorite outfits and even keep you warm on a cold day. Many of the pieces in this chapter use basic stitches such as single, half-double, double, triple crochet and cluster stitches. Even if you don't know what these stitches mean right off the bat, you can find instructions in a great many "How-To" crochet books for beginners, and you can even take classes at your local community college or yarn store. If you'd like to start off with an easier project, I'd suggest you try the **Bouclé Skull Cap with Glitter Edge** (see page 54), the **Lazy Daze E-Z Hat** (see page 64) or the **Flower Scarf** (see page 78). The most challenging designs are the **Luscious Blues Flower Scarf** (see page

72) and the **Puffy Flowers Scarf** (see page 74). If you need to whip up a quick fashion accent, try the **Spring Chicks and Baby Bunnies Corsage** (see page 60), **Geometric Earrings** (see page 104) or the **Striped Wristband** (see page 98). And, if you're on a long plane trip to Paris or Mongolia, you may have enough time to crochet the **Scarf Hoodie** (see page 96).

These designs are popular among all sorts of people, so don't be shy. Once you've learned the basic pattern, you can make your own unique designs by just changing colors and using different materials. Hey, your mother, daughter, grandmother and granddaughter might just like it! I'm delighted to share these designs with you.

bouclé skull cap with glitter edge

This hat is made with bouclé yarn and glitter yarn. Bouclé yarn is thick, bulky and very soft, which makes this project go quickly. Finishing the edge with glitter yarn makes this hat distinctive and a little spunky.

yarn

2 skeins Lion Brand Lion Bouclé (acrylic/mohair/nylon blend, 57 yds ea) in color #213 Taffy (MC)

1 skein Patons Brilliant (acrylic/nylon/polyester blend, 166 yds ea) in color #23 Gold Glow (CC)

hooks and notions

size I/9 (5.5mm) hook

If necessary, change hook size to obtain gauge.

yarn needle

gauge

11 dc x 4 rows = 4" (10cm)

finished size

19" (48cm) around x 7½" (19cm) tall

notes

Please refer to the individual patterns for instructions on which rounds should be joined.

HAT

With MC, ch 4, sl st in first ch to form ring.

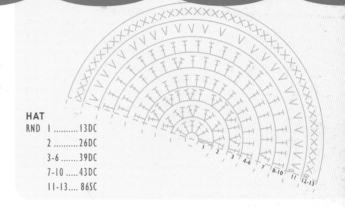

HAT

RND	
1	13DC
2	26DC
3-6	39DC
7-10	43DC
11-13	86SC

RND 1: Ch 3 (counts as first dc), work 12 dc into ring, place marker in last st to mark end of rnd. Do not join in first st—13 dc total.

RND 2: Work 2 dc in each st around, replace marker in last st throughout pattern—26 dc total.

RND 3: * Dc in next st, 2 dc in next st; rep from * around—39 dc total.

RNDS 4–6: Dc in each st around.

RND 7: Work * 2 dc in next st, dc in each of next 11 sts; rep from * twice, 2 dc in next st, dc in each of last 2 sts—43 dc total.

RNDS 8–10: Dc in each st around.
Sl st in next st. Fasten off, leaving a long tail.

RND 11: Beg 10 sts from last st worked, join CC, ch 1, work 2 sc in each dc around, sl st in first sc to join—86 sc total.

RNDS 12–13: Ch 1, sc in each st around.
Sl st in next st. Fasten off, leaving a long tail. Use a yarn needle to weave in ends.

sporty hat with a brim

The technique for this pattern is more intricate because of the addition of the brim. Not only will it help keep the sun out of your eyes, but you can customize it by putting a team's insignia on the front for your favorite sports fan.

yarn

2 skeins Lion Brand Wool-Ease (acrylic/wool/rayon blend, 197 yds ea) in color #112 Red Sprinkles

hooks and notions

size I/9 (5.5mm) hook

If necessary, change hook size to obtain gauge.

stitch marker

yarn needle

gauge

12 hdc x 5 rows = 4" (10cm) with 2 strands held together

finished size

19" (48cm) around x 8¼" (21cm) tall, including brim

notes

This pattern is worked in the round without joining. Place a marker in the last stitch of each round to mark the end of the round. Do not turn at the end of each round.

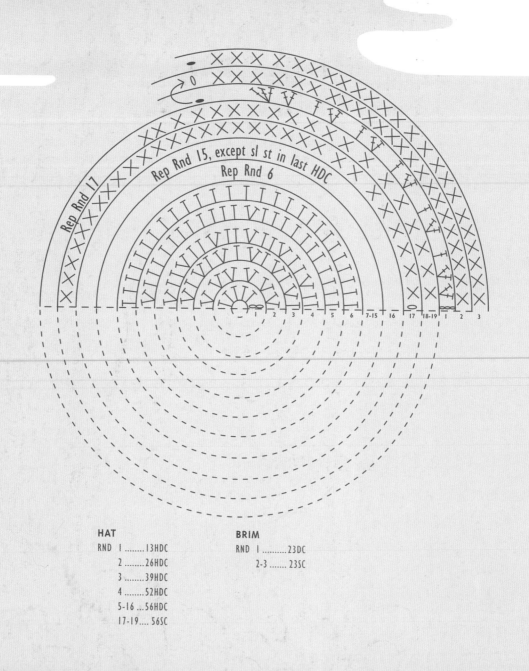

Rep Rnd 17

Rep Rnd 15, except sl st in last HDC

Rep Rnd 6

HAT

RND 1 ....13HDC
2 ....26HDC
3 ....39HDC
4 ....52HDC
5-16 ...56HDC
17-19.... 56SC

BRIM

RND 1 ....23DC
2-3 .... 23SC

HAT

With 2 strands of yarn held tog, ch 4, sl st in first ch to form ring.

RND 1: Ch 2 (counts as first hdc), work 12 hdc into ring, place marker in last st to mark end of rnd. Do not join in first st—13 hdc total.

RND 2: Work 2 hdc in each st around, replace marker in last st throughout pattern—26 hdc total.

RND 3: * Hdc in next st, 2 hdc in next st; rep from * around—39 hdc total.

RND 4: * Hdc in each of next 2 sts, 2 hdc in next st; rep from * around—52 hdc total.

RND 5: * Hdc in each of next 11 sts, 2 hdc in next st; rep from * 3 times, hdc in each of last 4 sts—56 hdc total.

RNDS 6–15: Hdc in each st around.

RND 16: Hdc in each st to last hdc, sl st in last hdc.

RNDS 17–19: Ch 1, sc in each st around, sl st in first sc to join.

BRIM

RND 1: Ch 3 (counts as first dc), 2 dc in each of next 2 sts, * dc in next st, 2 dc in next st; rep from * 4 times, 3 dc in next st, skip next 2 sts, sl st in next st, turn—23 dc total.

RND 2: Ch 1, sc in each dc across, skip next 2 sts from Rnd 19, sl st in next st, turn—23 sc total.

RND 3: Ch 1, sc in each sc across brim, sl st in beg ch-1. Fasten off, leaving a long tail. Use a yarn needle to weave in ends.

59

The corsage is a fun accent to any outfit. I like to use different yarns and colors to create my own daily bouquet of wearable flowers. The pearls in the center and the mohair yarn on my pattern remind me of spring chicks and baby bunnies.

yarn

1 skein Crystal Palace Yarns Kid Merino (kid mohair/merino wool/micro nylon blend, 240 yds ea) in color #4686 Strawberry Soda (MC)

1 skein Crystal Palace Yarns Kid Merino (kid mohair/merino wool/micro nylon blend, 240 yds ea) in color #4672 Berry (CC1)

1 skein Crystal Palace Yarns Kid Merino (kid mohair/merino wool/micro nylon blend, 240 yds ea) in color #4676 Pacific Blue (CC2)

hooks and notions

size C/2 (2.75mm) hook

If necessary, change hook size to obtain gauge.

yarn needle

25–35 6mm glass beads (Gutermann)

nylon beading thread

pin back

gauge

23 sc x 38 rows = 4" (10cm)

finished size

Large Flower

2" (5cm) in diameter

Small Flower

1½" (4cm) in diameter

Leaf

2" (5cm) in diameter

SMALL FLOWER (MAKE 4)

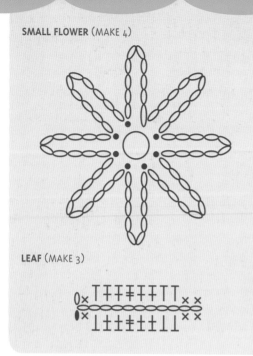

LEAF (MAKE 3)

SMALL FLOWER (make 4: 2 small flowers with MC and 2 small flowers with CC1)

With MC (or CC1) and leaving a 16" (41cm) tail, ch 4, sl st in first ch to form ring.

RND 1: Work (ch 10, sl st into ring) 8 times.

Fasten off, leaving a 16" (41cm) tail.

LARGE FLOWER (make 4: 2 large flowers with MC and 2 large flowers with CC1)

With MC (or CC1) and leaving a 16" (41cm) tail, ch 4, sl st in first ch to form ring.

RND 1: Ch 1, work 8 sc into ring, sl st in first sc to join.

RND 2: Work (ch 10, sl st in next sc) 8 times.

RND 3: *Work (ch 1, 2 sc, 2 hdc, 6 dc, 2 hdc, 2 sc, ch 1) in next ch-10 sp, sl st in next sl st; rep from * 7 more times, sl st in beg ch-1 to join.

Fasten off, leaving a 16" (41cm) tail.

LEAF (make 3)

With CC2 and leaving a 16" (41cm) tail, ch 12.

RND 1: Sc in second ch from hook, hdc in next st, dc in each of next 2 sts, trc in next st, dc in each of next 2 sts, hdc in each of next 2 sts, sc in each of next 2 sts, working around the bottom of the ch, sc in each of next 2 sts, hdc in each of next 2 sts, dc in each of next 2 sts, trc in next st, dc in each of next 2 sts, hdc in next st, sc in next st, sl st in skipped ch at beg of rnd—22 sts total.

Fasten off, leaving a 16" (41cm) tail.

LARGE FLOWER (MAKE 4)

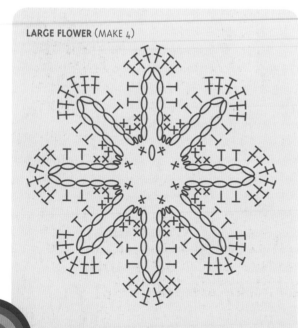

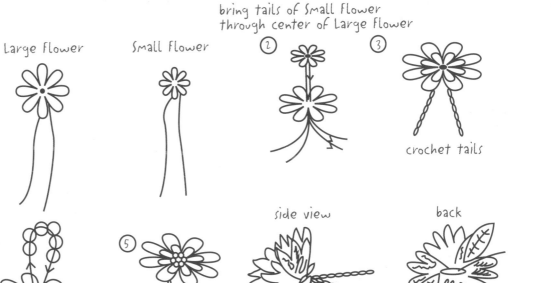

① Large Flower

Small Flower

bring tails of Small Flower
through center of Large Flower

② ③ crochet tails

④ sew beads into center of Corsage

⑤ side view back

add a pin back

Assembly

Place one Small Flower on top of one Large Flower, drawing all the tails through the center of the flowers and out the bottom. Repeat for the remaining three sets of flowers. Make chain stitches to the end of each tail and fasten off. Make chains for the ends of the Leaf tails and fasten off. Thread beads onto nylon beading thread and sew them to the center of each flower set. Arrange all four sets of flowers with leaves, bundling the chain tails together with a long strand of yarn. Secure a pin back with nylon beading thread to the back of the flowers, leaving the chain tails to hang below.

lazy daze e-z hat

This hat is great for beginners. Only single and double crochet stitches are used to make this hat. If you're an experienced crocheter, this is a good opportunity to make something fun while you are watching TV or just plain zoning out.

yarn

1 skein Lion Brand Yarn Moonlight Mohair (acrylic/mohair/cotton/metallic polyester blend, 82 yds ea) in color #207 Coral Reef

hooks and notions

size I/9 (5.5mm) hook

If necessary, change hook size to obtain gauge.

stitch marker

yarn needle

gauge

13 dc x 4½ rows = 4" (10cm)

finished size

20" (51cm) around x 8¼" (21cm) tall

notes

This pattern is worked in the round without joining. Place a marker in the last stitch of each round to mark the end of the round. Do not turn at the end of each round.

HAT

With MC, ch 4, sl st in first ch to form ring.

RND 1: Ch 3 (counts as first dc), work 12 dc into ring, place marker in last st to mark end of rnd. Do not join in first st—13 dc total.

RND 2: Work 2 dc in each st around, replace marker in last st throughout pattern—26 dc total.

RND 3: * Dc in next st, 2 dc in next st; rep from * around—39 dc total.

RND 4: * Dc in each of next 2 sts, 2 dc in next st; rep from * around—52 dc total.

RND 5: Dc in each st around.

RNDS 6–12: Rep Rnd 5.

RND 13: Dc in each st around to last st, sl st in last dc.

RND 14: Ch 1, sc in each st around, do not join in first sc—52 sc total.

RNDS 15–16: Sc in next st and in each st around. Fasten off, leaving a long tail. Use a yarn needle to weave in ends.

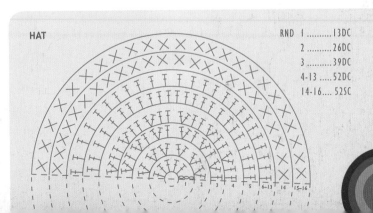

HAT

RND 1	13DC
2	26DC
3	39DC
4-13	52DC
14-16	52SC

your favorite you flower bag

This bag can be for your favorite girl or for your favorite you. It's a perfect on-the-go crochet kit to hold your latest project, needles, hooks and yarn! After making each part, fold the handle in half widthwise and sew together with woven seams. It's good to make sure the handles are placed correctly.

yarn

1 skein The Leader Aran (100% acrylic, 220 yds ea) in color #124 Yellow-Orange (MC)

1 skein The Leader Aran (100% acrylic, 220 yds ea) in color #129 Orange (CC1)

1 skein The Leader Aran (100% acrylic, 220 yds ea) in color #030 Light Yellow (CC2)

hooks and notions

size F/5 (3.75mm) hook

size D/3 (3.25mm) hook

If necessary, change hook size to obtain gauge.

stitch marker

yarn needle

gauge

16 sc x 10 rows = 4" (10cm) with larger hook

finished size

7½" (19cm) wide x 7" (18cm) tall, excluding handles

Flower measures 2" (5cm) in diameter

notes

This pattern is worked in the round without joining. Place a marker in the last stitch of each round to mark the end of the round. Do not turn at the end of each round.

BODY

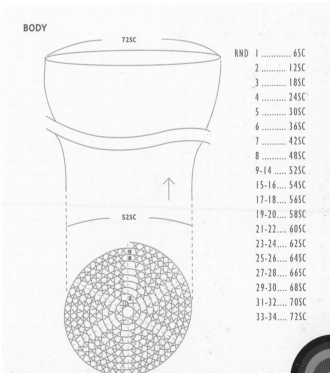

RND	
1	6SC
2	12SC
3	18SC
4	24SC
5	30SC
6	36SC
7	42SC
8	48SC
9-14	52SC
15-16	54SC
17-18	56SC
19-20	58SC
21-22	60SC
23-24	62SC
25-26	64SC
27-28	66SC
29-30	68SC
31-32	70SC
33-34	72SC

72SC

52SC

FLOWER

RND 1 .... 6SC
2 .... 12SC
3 ....6 PETALS

PURSE BODY

With larger hook and MC, ch 4, sl st in first ch to form ring.

RND 1: Ch 1, 6 sc into ring, place marker in last st to mark end of rnd. Do not join in first st—6 sc total.

RND 2: Work 2 sc in each st around, replace marker in last st throughout pattern—12 sc total.

RND 3: * Sc in next st, 2 sc in next st; rep from * around—18 sc total.

RND 4: * Sc in each of next 2 sts, 2 sc in next st; rep from * around—24 sc total.

RND 5: Sc in next st, 2 sc in next st, * sc in each of next 3 sts, 2 sc in next st; rep from * 4 times, sc in last st of rnd—30 sc total.

RND 6: * Sc in each of next 4 sts, 2 sc in next st; rep from * around—36 sc total.

RND 7: Sc in each of next 2 sts, 2 sc in next st, * sc in each of next 5 sts, 2 sc in next st; rep from * 4 times, sc in last st of rnd—42 sc total.

RND 8: * Sc in each of next 6 sts, 2 sc in next st; rep from * around—48 sc total.

RND 9: Sc in each of next 5 sts, 2 sc in next st, * sc in each of next 11 sts, 2 sc in next st; rep from * twice, sc in each of last 6 sts—52 sc total.

RNDS 10–14: Sc in each st around.

RND 15: Sc in each of first 12 sts, 2 sc in next st, sc in each of next 25 sts, 2 sc in next st, sc in each of last 13 sts—54 sc total.

RND 16: Rep Rnd 10.

RND 17: 2 sc in next st, sc in each of next 26 sts, 2 sc in next st, sc in each st around—56 sc total.

RND 18: Rep Rnd 10.

RND 19: Sc in each of next 6 sts, 2 sc in next st, sc in each of next 27 sts, 2 sc in next st, sc in each st around—58 sc total.

RND 20: Rep Rnd 10.

RND 21: Sc in each of next 21 sts, 2 sc in next st, sc in each of next 28 sts, 2 sc in next st, sc in each st around—60 sc total.

RND 22: Rep Rnd 10.

RND 23: Sc in each of next 4 sts, 2 sc in next st, sc in each of next 39 sts, 2 sc in next st, sc in each st around—62 sc total.

RND 24: Rep Rnd 10.

RND 25: 2 sc in next st, sc in each of next 30 sts, 2 sc in next st, sc in each st around—64 sc total.

RND 26: Rep Rnd 10.

RND 27: Sc in each of next 7 sts, 2 sc in next st, sc in each of next 31 sts, 2 sc in next st, sc in each st around—66 sc total.

RND 28: Rep Rnd 10.

RND 29: Sc in each of next 24 sts, 2 sc in next st, sc in each of next 32 sts, 2 sc in next st, sc in each st around—68 sc total.

RND 30: Rep Rnd 10.

RND 31: Sc in each of next 16 sts, 2 sc in next st, sc in each of next 33 sts, 2 sc in next st, sc in each st around—70 sc total.

RND 32: Rep Rnd 10.

RND 33: 2 sc in next st, sc in each of next 34 sts, 2 sc in next st, sc in each st around—72 sc total.

RND 34: Rep Rnd 10.

Fasten off. Use a yarn needle to weave in ends.

HANDLES (make 2)

With larger hook and MC, ch 47.

ROW 1: Sc in second ch from hook and in each ch across, turn—46 sc total.

ROWS 2–6: Ch 1, sc in each st across, turn.

Fasten off. Use a yarn needle to weave in ends.

Fold in half widthwise and sew long edges together (see diagram at right).

FLOWER (make 4)

With smaller hook and CC1, ch 3, sl st in first ch to form ring.

RND 1: Work 6 sc into ring, sl st in first sc to join.

RND 2: Ch 1, 2 sc in each st around, sl st in first sc to join—12 sc total.

Fasten off.

RND 3: With CC2 in any st from previous rnd, * work (ch 3, 3 dc, drop loop from hook, insert hook in top of ch-3, pick up dropped loop and draw through loop on hook, ch 3, sl st) 6 times around—6 petals.

Fasten off, leaving a long tail for sewing.

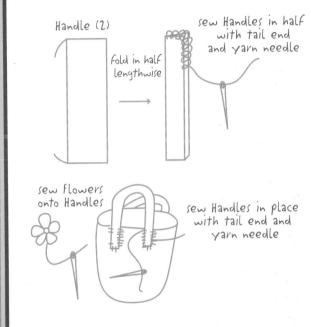

Handle (2)

Fold in half lengthwise

sew Handles in half with tail end and yarn needle

sew flowers onto Handles

sew Handles in place with tail end and yarn needle

Finishing

Turn the bag inside out, and pin about 1½" (4cm) of both ends of one Handle to the inside of the bag, approximately 2" (5cm) in from each side of the bag. Sew the Handle ends to the inside of the bag with a yarn needle and MC. Repeat for the remaining Handle on the other side of the bag. Turn the bag right side out and sew a Flower over each Handle using a yarn needle and CC2 to match the center of each Flower.

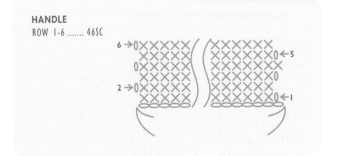

HANDLE

ROW 1-6 .... 46SC

In this project, you can learn or practice how to join motifs together. It seems more complicated than it is. Just slip-stitch into the corresponding place of the adjoining motif and then work the appropriate stitches in the motif that's in progress. Rinse and repeat.

yarn

1 skein Tahki Yarns Cotton Classic (100% mercerized cotton, 108 yds ea) in color #3703 Green (MC)

1 skein Tahki Yarns Cotton Classic (100% mercerized cotton, 108 yds ea) color #3713 Meadow (CC)

hooks and notions

size F/5 (3.75mm) hook

If necessary, change hook size to obtain gauge.

yarn needle

gauge

16 sc x 15 rows = 4" (10cm)

finished size

4" (10cm) wide x 52½" (133cm) long

green tones flower scarf

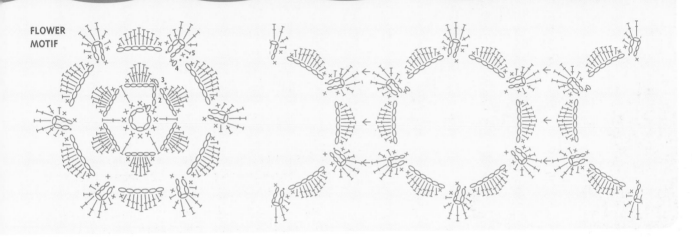

FLOWER MOTIF

MOTIF (make 12)

With MC, ch 6, sl st in first ch to form ring.

RND 1: Ch 1, 12 sc into ring, sl st in first sc to join—12 sc total.

RND 2: Ch 8 (counts as dc, ch 5), * skip next st, dc in next st, ch 5; rep from * around, sl st in 3rd ch of beg ch-5 to join—6 ch-5 spaces.

RND 3: Ch 1, work (sc, hdc, 5 dc, hdc, sc) into each ch-5 sp around, sl st in beg ch-1 to join—6 petals total.

RND 4: Switch to CC, ch 1, sc in same space as sl st, * ch 6, sl st in same sc to make loop, ch 6, sk next 9 sts (1 petal), sc in sp between petals; rep from * around, sl st in first sc to join.

RND 5: Work (sc, hdc, 5 dc, hdc, sc) into first ch-6 loop, (sc, hdc, 7 dc, hdc, sc) into next ch-6 sp; rep around, sl st in first sc to join.

Assembly

Crochet each motif to the next one while crocheting Rnd 5, working in slip stitch. Follow the arrows in the diagram above to see where the slip stitches are attached to the adjacent motifs.

SPECIAL STITCHES

5-dc Cluster: Yo, insert hook in st, yo, pull through st, yo, pull through 2 lps on hook, (yo, insert hook in same st, yo, pull through st, yo, pull through 2 lps on hook) 4 times, yo, pull through all lps on hook, ch 1.

2-dc Cluster: Yo, insert hook in st, yo, pull through st, yo, pull through 2 lps on hook, yo, insert hook in same st, yo, pull through st, yo, pull through 2 lps on hook, yo, pull through all lps on hook, ch 1.

This pattern is a challenging project for a beginner. If you can get comfortable with joining motifs together, the other challenge is the delicacy of the mohair yarn. The finished product turns out to be a lovely, lightweight and luscious scarf. Definitely worth the effort.

yarn

2 skeins/balls Crystal Palace Yarns Kid Merino (kid mohair/merino wool/micro nylon blend, 240 yds ea) in color #4676 Pacific Blue (MC)

2 skeins/balls Crystal Palace Yarns Kid Merino (kid mohair/merino wool/mictro nylon blend, 240 yds ea) in color #4681 Misty Blue (C)

hooks and notions

size D/3 (3.25mm) hook

If necessary, change hook size to obtain gauge.

yarn needle

gauge

19 sc x 33 rows = 4" (10cm)

finished size

6½" (17cm) wide x 63" (160cm) long

Each flower measures 3½" (9cm) in diameter

luscious blues
flower scarf

MOTIF A (make 14)

With MC, ch 4, sl st in first ch to form ring.

RND 1: Ch 3 (counts as first dc), 15 dc into ring, sl st in 3rd ch of beg ch-3 to join—16 dc total.

RND 2: * Ch 4, 5-dc cluster in next st, ch 4, sl st in next st; rep from * around, sl st in 1st ch of beg ch-4 to join—8 clusters total.

RND 3: Change to CC, sl st in each of next 3 ch, ch 1, * sc in top of next cluster, ch 5; rep from * around, sl st in first sc to join—8 ch-5 spaces total.

RND 4: * Ch 3, work ([2-dc cluster, ch 2] three times) in each ch-5 sp around, sl st in 3rd ch of beg ch-3 to join.

RND 5: Ch 1, * sc in next cluster, ch 5; rep from * around, sl st in beg ch-1 to join.

MOTIF B (make 14)

Work as for Motif A, reversing colors.

FLOWER MOTIF

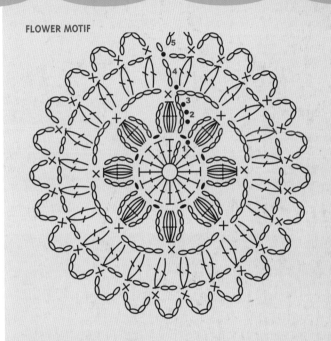

Assembly

In the final round (Rnd 5) of each flower motif, use a slip stitch to link one motif to the next, following the arrows in the diagram to see how the motifs are linked together. You will link a total of 14 Motif A and 14 Motif B.

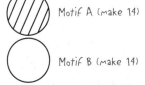

— 28 Motifs total —

Motif A (make 14)

Motif B (make 14)

puffy flowers scarf

This elaborate project involves more than just crocheting. After making all the lively flowers, there is an intricate design to connect them together. The flowers, chains and end motifs make this scarf delicate and charming. I know from experience the wearer feels like royalty.

yarn

2 skeins Crystal Palace Yarn Merino Frapp (80% merino/20% nylon, 140 yds ea) in color #143 heathered red (MC)

2 skeins Crystal Palace Yarn Merino Frapp (80% merino/20% nylon, 140 yds ea) in color #29B heathered mauve (CC1)

2 skeins Crystal Palace Yarn Merino Frapp (80% merino/20% nylon, 140 yds ea) in color #146 heathered purple (CC2)

1 skein each Crystal Palace Yarns Kid Merino (merino/kid mohair/micro nylon blend, 240 yds ea) in color #4686 Strawberry Soda (CC3) and #4672 Berry (CC4)

hooks and notions

size F/5 (3.75mm) hook

If necessary, change hook size to obtain gauge.

yarn needle

gauge

15 sc x 12 rows = 4" (10cm) with MC

finished size

64" (163cm) long

Each flower measures 3½" (9cm) in diameter

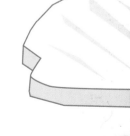

MOTIF A (make 14)

With MC, ch 4, sl st in first ch to form ring.

RND 1: Ch 3 (counts as dc), 11 dc into ring, sl st in 3rd ch of beg ch-3 to join—12 dc total.

RND 2: Ch 6 (counts as dc, ch 3), dc in same st as join, work (dc, ch 3, dc) in each st around, sl st in 3rd ch of beg ch-6 to join—24 dc total.

RND 3: Ch 3, * 3 dc in ch-3 sp, ch 3, sc in sp between next 2 dc sts, ch 3; rep from * around, sl st in 3rd ch to join—12 groups of 3 dc total.

Fasten off, leaving a long tail. Weave in all ends.

MOTIF B (make 14)

With CC1, work as for Motif A.

MOTIF C (make 14)

With CC2, work as for Motif A.

MOTIF D (make 6)

With CC3 and CC4 held together, ch 4, sl st in first ch to form ring.

RND 1: Ch 3 (counts as dc), 11 dc into ring, sl st in 3rd ch of beg ch-3 to join—12 dc total.

Do not fasten off.

FLOWER MOTIFS A–C

FLOWER MOTIF D

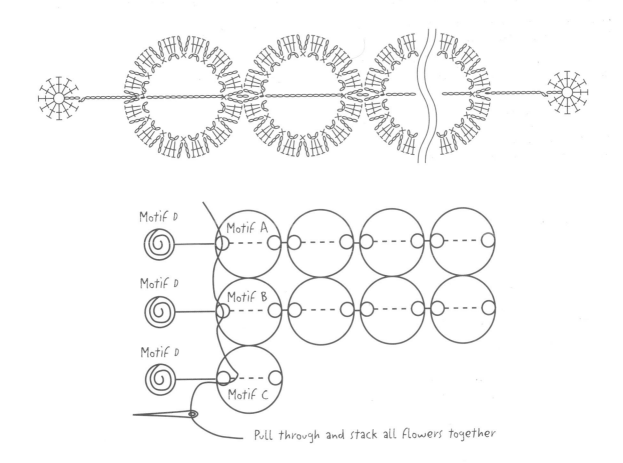

Pull through and stack all flowers together

Finishing

Attach CC3 in any st of one Motif D, ch 10, sc in any sc (between dc groups) of Motif A. * Ch 13, sc in sc on opposite side of same Motif A, ch 2, sc in any sc of next Motif A; rep from * until all 16 of Motif A are joined. Ch 10, sl st in any st of second Motif D.

Join all of Motif B in one strip and all of Motif C in one strip in the same manner as Motif A.

Lay strips of A and B next to each other with WS facing. Lay strip of C with RS facing on top between A and B. Sew all three strips together. Weave in any loose ends.

flower hat and scarf set

This flapper-style hat can be made very easily. Make sure to leave long loose ends when you make the flower to weave it more easily onto the hat. Some fun color combinations to try are a moss green hat with an ivory flower or a chocolate hat with a pink flower. The matching scarf is made with a half-double crochet stitch all the way across. It's so simple to make, but the slip-on flower makes this scarf very original.

yarn

Hat and Scarf

3 skeins Lion Brand Wool-Ease (acrylic/wool blend, 197 yds ea) in color #153 Black (MC)

1 skein for Hat; 2 skeins for Scarf

1 skein Red Heart Super Saver (100% acrylic, 364 yds ea) in color #378 Claret for flowers (CC)

hooks and notions

size G/6 (4.50mm) hook (for Hat)

size I/9 (5.50mm) hook (for Scarf)

size F/5 (3.75mm) hook (for Flowers)

If necessary, change hook size to obtain gauge.

yarn needle

stitch markers

gauge

Hat

15 dc and 6 rows = 4" (10cm) on size G/6 (4.50mm) hook

Scarf

12 hdc and 6 rows = 4" (10cm) on size I/9 (5.50mm) with two strands of MC held together

finished sizes

Hat

24" (61cm) around x 9" (23cm) tall

Scarf

71" (180cm) long x 4" (10cm) wide

Flower

4" (10cm) in diameter (for Scarf & Hat)

notes

The hat pattern is worked in the round without joining. Place a marker in the last stitch of each round to mark the end of the round. Do not turn at the end of each round.

HAT

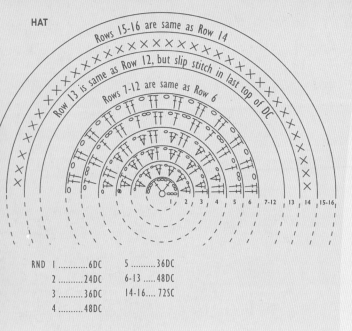

Rows 15-16 are same as Row 14

Rows 13 is same as Row 12, but slip stitch in last top of DC

Rows 7-12 are same as Row 6

1	2	3	4	5	6	7-12	13	14	15-16

RND 1 ....6DC	5 ....36DC	
2 ....24DC	6-13 .....48DC	
3 ....36DC	14-16.... 72SC	
4 ....48DC		

RND 2: Work 2 dc in 3rd ch of beg ch-6 on first row, ch 1, sk 1 ch, 2 dc in next ch, ch 1, sk 1 ch, * 2 dc in next dc, ch 1, sk 1 ch, 2 dc in next ch, ch 1, sk 1 ch, *; rep between * 4 more times—24 dc total.

RND 3: * Dc in next st, 2 dc in next st, ch 1, sk 1 ch *; rep between * around—36 dc total.

RND 4: * Dc in each of next 2 sts, 2 dc in next st, ch 1, sk 1 ch *; rep between * around—48 dc total.

RND 5: * Dc in each of next 2 sts, ch 2, sk 1 dc, dc in next st, ch 1, sk 1 ch *; rep between * around—36 dc total.

RND 6: * Dc in each of next 2 sts, ch 1, sk 1 ch, dc in next ch, dc in next dc, ch 1, sk 1 ch *; rep between * around—48 dc total.

RNDS 7–12: * Dc in each of next 2 sts, ch 1, sk 1 ch *; rep between * around.

RND 13: Rep Row 12, ending sl st in first dc of rnd.

RNDS 14–16: Ch 1, sc in each st and ch around, sl st in first sc to join—72 sc.

Fasten off. Use a yarn needle to weave in tail ends.

HAT

With G/6 (4.50mm) hook and MC, ch 4, sl st in first ch to form ring.

RND 1: Ch 6 (counts as dc, ch 3) * dc into ring, ch 3 *; rep between * 4 more times, do not join in beg of rnd—6 ch-3 loops total.

FLOWER

Leave approx a 19" (48cm) tail to sew the flower onto the hat. With size F/5 (3.75mm) hook and CC, ch 4, sl st in first ch to form ring.

RND 1: Ch 5 (counts as 1 dc, ch 2), * dc into ring, ch 2 *, rep between * 4 more times, sl st in 3rd ch of beg ch-5 to join—6 ch-2 lps.

RND 2: Ch 1, work (sc, 2 hdc, dc, 2 hdc, sc) into each ch-2 sp around, sl st in first sc to join, turn (6 petals).

RND 3: (Ch 3, sl st) in between petals from previous row 5 times, ch 3, sl st in first ch of beg ch-3, turn.

RND 4: Ch 1, work (sc, 2 hdc, 3 dc, 2 hdc, sc) into each ch-3 sp around, sl st in first sc to join, turn.

RND 5: (Ch 4, sl st) in between petals from previous row 5 times, ch 3, sl st in first ch of beg ch-4, turn.

RND 6: Ch 1, work (sc, 3 hdc, 4 dc, 3 hdc, sc) into each ch-4 sp around, sl st in first sc to join.

Fasten off. Sew flower to hat. Using needle, weave in tail ends.

SCARF

With I/9 (5.50mm) hook and two strands of MC held together, ch 150.

ROW 1: Hdc in 3rd ch from hook and in each ch across, turn—148 hdc total.

ROWS 2–6: Ch 2, hdc in each st across, turn.

Fasten off, leaving a 10" (25cm) tail. Use a yarn needle to weave in ends.

FRINGE

Cut 48 10" (25cm) strands of MC. Hold four strands together, and fold them in half. Use hook to pull fold through edge of scarf at the end of each row. Pull fringe ends through the folded loop. Pull to tighten. Attach fringe to each row on both ends of Scarf. Trim fringe evenly.

FLOWER

Create a second flower, as for the Hat Flower, but keep working until the Flower measures 4" (10cm) in diameter.

Band

With F/5 (3.75mm) hook and CC, ch 11.

ROW 1: Sc in second ch from hook, turn.

ROWS 2–4: Ch 1, sc in each st across, turn.

Fasten off, leaving a 10" (25cm) tail. Using yarn needle, weave in ends. Sew the band onto the back of the flower.

SCARF

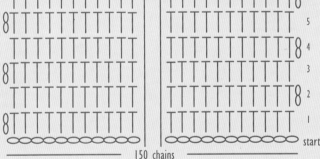

150 chains

FLOWER (FOR HAT & SCARF)

FLOWER BAND

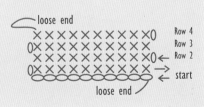

loose end
Row 4
Row 3
Row 2
start
loose end

Flower

sew flower onto Hat

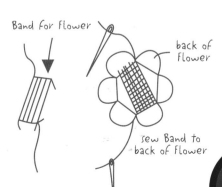

Band for Flower

back of Flower

sew Band to back of Flower

disco glitter hat

This hat is made with double crochet and shell stitch. Typically, shell stitches are used for edging. Using this stitch and the funky yarn makes the hat an original piece. Who needs a disco ball when you have glittery yarn?

yarn

1 skein Patons Brilliant (acrylic/nylon/polyester blend, 166 yds ea) in color #3314 Lilac Luster

hooks and notions

size I/9 (5.5mm) hook

If necessary, change hook size to obtain gauge.

yarn needle

stitch marker

gauge

13 dc x 6½ rows = 4" (10cm)

finished size

23" (58cm) around x 8" (20cm) tall

notes

This pattern is worked in the round without joining. Place a marker in the last stitch of each round to mark the end of the round. Do not turn at the end of each round.

HAT

With MC, ch 4, sl st in first ch to form ring.

RND 1: Ch 3 (counts as first dc), work 12 dc into ring, place marker in last st to mark end of rnd. Do not join in first st—13 dc total.

RND 2: Work 2 dc in each st around, replace marker in last st throughout pattern—26 dc total.

RND 3: * Dc in next st, 2 dc in next st; rep from * around—39 dc total.

RND 4: * Dc in each of next 2 sts, 2 dc in next st; rep from * around—52 dc total.

RND 5: * Dc in each of next 3 sts, 2 dc in next st; rep from * around—65 dc total.

RND 6: * Sk 2 sts, 5 dc in next st, sk 2 sts, sc in next st; rep from * around, ending sk 1 st, sc in last st.

RND 7: * Sk first 2 dc of next 5-dc group, sc in next dc (center of 5-dc group), sk next 2 dc, 5 dc in next sc; rep from * around.

RNDS 8–13: Cont in a spiral, working sc in 3rd dc of each 5-dc group and 5 dc in each sc.

Sl st in next st. Fasten off, leaving a long tail for weaving in ends. Use a yarn needle to weave in ends.

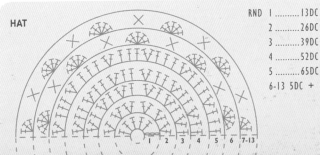

HAT

RND 1 ....13DC
2 ....26DC
3 ....39DC
4 ....52DC
5 ....65DC
6-13 5DC + 1SC ALL AROUND

snowball fight
mittens

This design is great for snowball fights. I suggest you make the thumb part first. When you are ready to attach the thumb, turn the thumb inside out before you single crochet in the first seven stitches. Follow the instructions and once the mitten body is done, you can finish attaching the thumb with woven seams for the remaining eleven stitches.

yarn

1 skein Dale of Norway Dale Baby Ull (100% wool, 192 yds ea) in color #9436 Kiwi (MC)

1 skein Dale of Norway Dale Baby Ull (100% wool, 192 yds ea) in color #20 Off White (CC)

hooks and notions

size F/5 (3.75mm) hook

If necessary, change hook size to obtain gauge.

stitch marker

yarn needle

gauge

21 sc x 19 rows = 4" (10cm)

finished size

7½" (19cm) long x 6½" (17cm) around wrist

Thumbs measure 2½" (6cm) long

notes

This pattern is worked in the round without joining. Place a marker in the last stitch of each round to mark the end of the round. Do not turn at the end of each round.

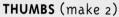

THUMBS

THUMBS

18SC

18

10

5

Thumb

19SC

RND	1	5SC
	2	10SC
	3-8	15SC
	9-18	18SC

SPECIAL STITCH

Dec: insert hook in next st, yo and draw up loop, insert hook in following st, yo and draw up loop, yo and draw through all 3 loops on hook.

THUMBS (make 2)

With CC, ch 3, sl st in first ch to form ring.

RND 1: Ch 1, 5 sc into ring, place marker in last st to mark end of rnd. Do not join in first st—5 sc total.

RND 2: Work 2 sc in each sc around, replace marker in last st throughout pattern—10 sc total.

RND 3: * Sc in next st, 2 sc in next st; rep from * around—15 sc total.

RND 4: Sc in each st around.

RNDS 5–8: Rep Rnd 4.

RND 9: * Sc in each of the next 4 sts, 2 sc in next st; rep from * around—18 sc total.

RNDS 10–18: Rep Rnd 4.

Sl st in next st. Fasten off, leaving a 10" (25cm) tail. Use a yarn needle to weave in ends.

BODY (make 2)

With MC, ch 4, sl st in first ch to form ring.

RND 1: Ch 1, 10 sc into ring, place marker in last st to mark end of rnd. Do not join in first st—10 sc total.

RND 2: Work 2 sc in each sc around, replace marker in last st throughout pattern—20 sc total.

RNDS 3–4: Sc in each st around.

RND 5: * Sc in next st, 2 sc in next st; rep from * around—30 sc total.

RNDS 6–7: Rep Rnd 3.

RND 8: * Sc in each of next 2 sts, 2sc in next st; rep from * around—40 sc total.

RNDS 9–17: Rep Rnd 3.

RND 18: * 2 sc in next st, sc in each of next 19 sts; rep from * once—42 sc total.

RNDS 19–36: Rep Rnd 3.

Join Thumb to Body

Turn Thumb inside out.

RND 37: With Thumb and Body held together and working through both thicknesses, sc in each of next 7 sts. Working in Body only, sc in each st around—42 sc total.

RND 38: Skip first 7 sc and ch 11 (rem Thumb sts). Working in Body only, sc in each st around—48 sc total.

RNDS 39–43: Rep Body Rnd 3—48 sc.

RND 44: Dec, sc in each of next 19 sts, dec, sc in each rem st around—46 sc total.

RNDS 45–46: Rep Rnd 3.

RND 47: Rep Rnd 44—44 sc total.

RNDS 48–56: Rep Rnd 3.

Sl st in next st. Fasten off, leaving a 10" (25cm) tail. Use a yarn needle to weave in ends. With MC and yarn needle, sew Thumb onto the ch 11 space at Rnd 38.

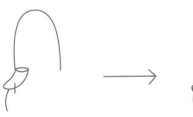

attach Thumb to Mitten Body at Rnd 37 (the first 7 sc)

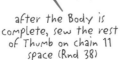

after the Body is complete, sew the rest of Thumb on chain 11 space (Rnd 38)

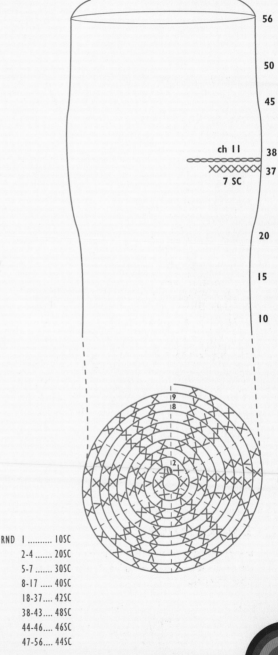

BODY

44 SC

56

50

45

ch 11   38

37

7 SC

20

15

10

19
18

12

RND 1	10 SC
2-4	20 SC
5-7	30 SC
8-17	40 SC
18-37	42 SC
38-43	48 SC
44-46	46 SC
47-56	44 SC

romantic
mohair hat

This hat has a romantic spirit. The mohair yarn gives it a lovely feel, and the brim is made with a chain of loops that softens the hat. Place the flower over the area where you change to a different color to mask the color flaw.

yarn

1 skein Classic Elite La Gran (mohair/wool/nylon blend, 90 yds ea) in color #6542 Lavender Ice (MC)

1 skein Classic Elite La Gran (mohair/wool/nylon blend, 90 yds ea) in color #6554 French Lilac (CC)

hooks and notions

size I/9 (5.5mm) hook

If necessary, change hook size to obtain gauge.

stitch marker

yarn needle

gauge

13 dc x 5 rows = 4" (10cm)

finished size

21½" (55cm) around x 10" (25cm) tall, including brim

Flower measures 4" (10cm) in diameter

notes

This pattern is worked in the round without joining. Place a marker in the last stitch of each round to mark the end of the round. Do not turn at the end of each round.

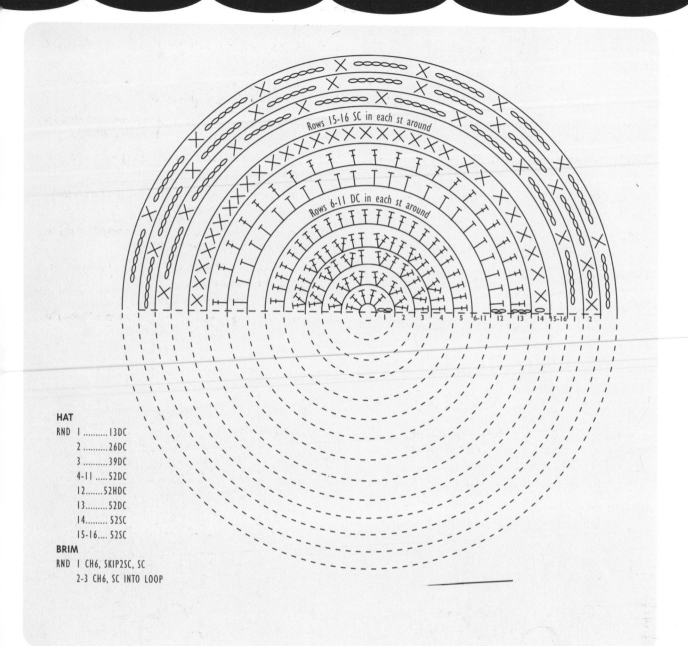

Rows 15-16 SC in each st around

Rows 6-11 DC in each st around

HAT

RND 1 ....13DC

2 ....26DC

3 ....39DC

4-11 .....52DC

12.......52HDC

13..........52DC

14......... 52SC

15-16.... 52SC

BRIM

RND 1 CH6, SKIP2SC, SC

2-3 CH6, SC INTO LOOP

HAT

With MC, ch 4, sl st in first ch to form ring.

RND 1: Ch 3 (counts as first dc), work 12 dc into ring, place marker in last st to mark end of rnd. Do not join in first st—13 dc total.

RND 2: Work 2 dc in each st around, replace marker in last st throughout pattern—26 dc total.

RND 3: * Dc in next st, 2 dc in next st; rep from * around—39 dc total.

RND 4: * Dc in each of next 2 sts, 2 dc in next st; rep from * around—52 dc total.

RNDS 5–11: Dc in each st around to last dc.
Sl st in next st. Fasten off, leaving a long tail.

RND 12: Joining CC, ch 2 (counts as hdc), hdc in each st around, sl st in 2nd ch of beg ch-2 to join.
Fasten off, leaving a long tail.

RND 13: Joining MC, ch 3 (counts as dc), dc in each st around, sl st in 3rd ch of beg ch-3 to join.

RNDS 14–16: Ch 1, sc in each st around, sl st in first sc to join.
Do not fasten off.

BRIM

RND 1: Ch 6, sk first 2 sts, sc in next st, *ch 6, sk next 2 sts, sc in next st; rep from * around, ending sc in second to last st. Do not join to beg of rnd.

RNDS 2–3: *Ch 6, sc into next ch-6 sp; rep from * around.
Fasten off, leaving a long tail. Use a yarn needle to weave in ends.

FLOWER

With CC, leave an approx 19" (48cm) tail at the beg, ch 4, sl st in first ch to form ring.

RND 1: Ch 5 (counts as dc and 2 chs), * dc into ring, ch 2; rep from * 4 times, sl st in 1st ch of beg ch-5 to join.

RND 2: Ch 1, work (sc, 2 hdc, dc, 2 hdc, sc) into each ch-2 sp around, sl st in first sc to join, turn—6 petals total.

RND 3: Working behind petals, (ch 3, sl st between petals) 6 times, sl st in 1st ch of beg ch-3 to join, turn.

RND 4: Ch 1, work (sc, 2 hdc, 3 dc, 2 hdc, sc) into each ch-3 sp around, sl st in first sc to join, turn.

RND 5: Working behind petals, (ch 4, sl st between petals) 6 times, sl st in 1st ch of beg ch-4 to join, turn.

RND 6: Ch 1, work (sc, 3 hdc, 4 dc, 3 hdc, sc) into each ch-4 sp around, sl st in first sc to join.
Fasten off, leaving a long tail for sewing.

Use a yarn needle to sew the flower to the hat. Weave in ends to finish.

FLOWER

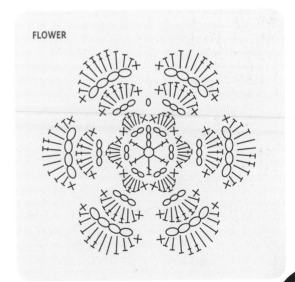

matching mother-daughter hats

This is a great pattern for a special mother-daughter outing. I prefer to use a multicolor, bulky yarn. And both hats can be made in three hours. A little tip: A mannequin head can be used to help put on the flower.

yarn

3 skeins Lion Brand Yarn Landscapes (wool/acrylic blend, 55 yds ea) in #271 Rose Garden

2 skeins for Mother Hat; 1 skein for Daughter Hat

hooks and notions

size I/9 (5.5mm) hook

size G/6 (4.50mm) hook

If necessary, change hook size to obtain gauge.

stitch marker

yarn needle

gauge

12 dc x 4 rows = 4" (10cm) with larger hook

15 dc x 4½ rows = 4" (10cm) with smaller hook

finished size

Mother Hat

22" (56cm) around x 9½" (24cm) tall

Flower measures 4" (10cm) in diameter

Daughter Hat

18" (46cm) around x 6½" (17cm) tall

Flower measures 3½" (9cm) in diameter

notes

This pattern is worked in the round without joining. Place a marker in the last stitch of each round to mark the end of the round. Do not turn at the end of each round.

MOTHER HAT

With larger hook, ch 4, form ring by joining with sl st to the 4th ch from hook.

RND 1: Ch 3 (counts as first dc), work 12 dc into ring, place marker in last st to mark end of rnd. Do not join in first st—13 dc total.

RND 2: Work 2 dc in each st around, replace marker in last st throughout pattern—26 dc total.

RND 3: * Dc in next st, 2 dc in next st; rep from * around—39 dc total.

RND 4: * Dc in each of next 2 sts, 2 dc in next st; rep from * around—52 dc total.

RNDS 5–9: Dc in each st around.

RND 10: Dc in each st around to last st, sl st in last st.

RND 11: Ch 3, dc in each st around, sl st in 3rd ch of beg ch-3.

RNDS 12–14: Ch 1, sc in each st around, sl st in first sc to join. Fasten off, leaving a long tail. Use a yarn needle to weave in ends.

FLOWER (for Mother Hat)

Leaving an approx 19" (48cm) tail, with larger hook ch 4, sl st in first ch to form ring.

RND 1: Ch 5 (counts as dc, ch 2), work (dc, ch 2) into ring 5 times, sl st in 3rd ch of beg ch-5 to join.

RND 2: Ch 1, work (sc, 2 hdc, dc, 2 hdc, sc) into each ch-2 space around, sl st in first sc to join, turn.

RND 3: Working behind petals, (ch 3, sl st) 5 times, ch 3, sl st in first ch of beg ch-3, turn.

RND 4: Ch 1, work (sc, 2 hdc, 3 dc, 2 hdc, sc) into each ch-3 sp around, sl st in first sc to join.

Fasten off, leaving a long tail for sewing.

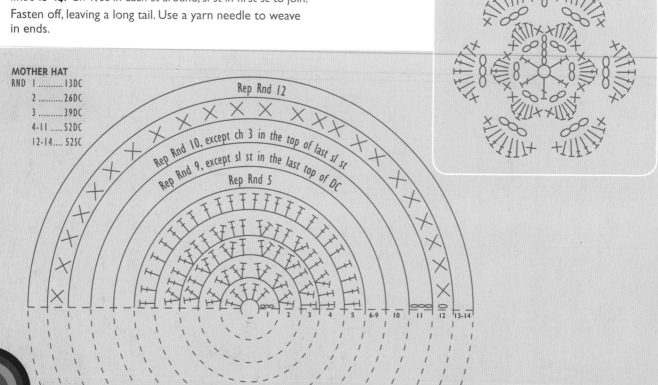

MOTHER HAT FLOWER

MOTHER HAT

RND 1	13 DC
2	26 DC
3	39 DC
4-11	52 DC
12-14	52 SC

Rep Rnd 12

Rep Rnd 10, except ch 3 in the top of last sl st

Rep Rnd 9, except sl st in the last top of DC

Rep Rnd 5

DAUGHTER HAT

With smaller hook, ch 4, sl st in first ch to form ring.

RND 1: Ch 3 (counts as first dc), work 11 dc into ring, place marker in last st to mark end of rnd. Do not join in first st—12 dc total.

RND 2: Work 2 dc in each st around, replace marker in last st throughout pattern—24 dc total.

RND 3: * Dc in next st, 2 dc in next st; rep from * around—36 dc total.

RND 4: * Dc in each of next 2 sts, 2 dc in next st; rep from * around—48 dc total.

RNDS 5–7: Dc in each st around.

RND 8: Dc in each st to last st, sl st in last st.

RND 9: Ch 1, sc in each st around, sl st in first sc to join.

RNDS 10–11: Ch 1, sc in each st around, sl st in first sc to join. Fasten off, leaving a long tail. Use a yarn needle to weave in ends.

FLOWER (for Daughter Hat)

Leaving an approx 15" (38cm) tail end, with smaller hook ch 4, sl st in first ch to form ring.

RND 1: Ch 5 (counts as dc, ch 2), work (dc, ch 2) into ring 5 times, sl st in 3rd ch of beg ch-5 to join.

RND 2: Ch 1, work (sc, 2 hdc, dc, 2 hdc, sc) into each ch-2 space around, sl st in first sc to join.

Fasten off, leaving a long tail for sewing.

Assembly

For both Mother and Daughter Hats, use the long tail from the Flower and a yarn needle to sew the Flower to the hat. Weave in ends.

DAUGHTER HAT FLOWER

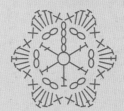

DAUGHTER HAT

RND	
1	12DC
2	24DC
3	36DC
4-8	48DC
9-11	48SC

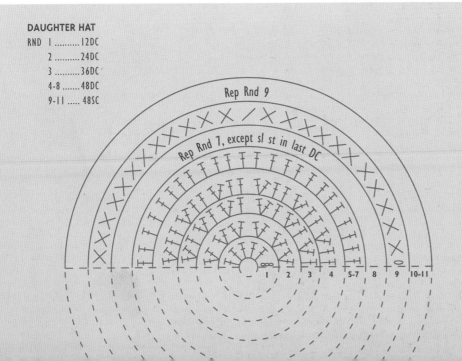

Rep Rnd 9

Rep Rnd 7, except sl st in last DC

1 2 3 4 5-7 8 9 10-11

95

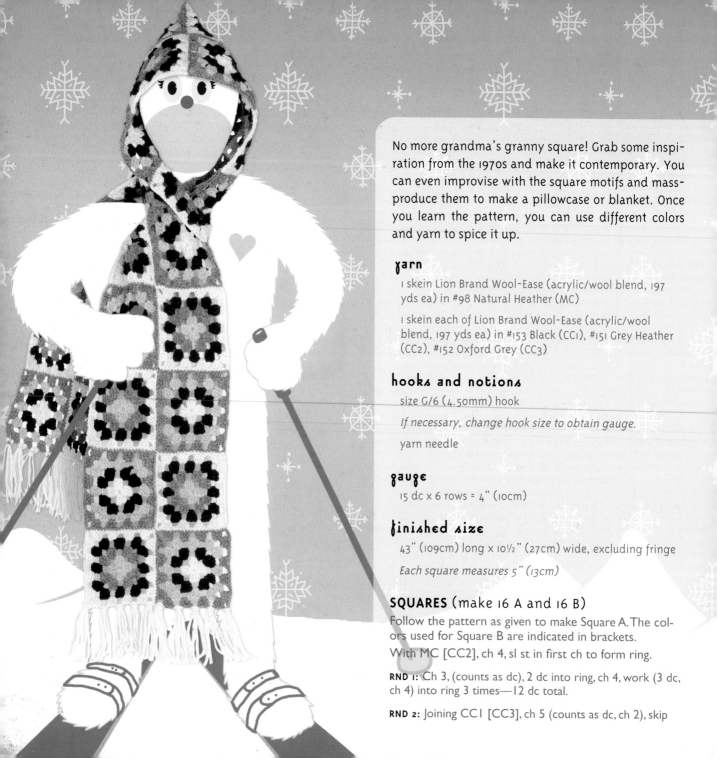

No more grandma's granny square! Grab some inspiration from the 1970s and make it contemporary. You can even improvise with the square motifs and mass-produce them to make a pillowcase or blanket. Once you learn the pattern, you can use different colors and yarn to spice it up.

yarn

1 skein Lion Brand Wool-Ease (acrylic/wool blend, 197 yds ea) in #98 Natural Heather (MC)

1 skein each of Lion Brand Wool-Ease (acrylic/wool blend, 197 yds ea) in #153 Black (CC1), #151 Grey Heather (CC2), #152 Oxford Grey (CC3)

hooks and notions

size G/6 (4.50mm) hook

If necessary, change hook size to obtain gauge.

yarn needle

gauge

15 dc x 6 rows = 4" (10cm)

finished size

43" (109cm) long x 10½" (27cm) wide, excluding fringe

Each square measures 5" (13cm)

SQUARES (make 16 A and 16 B)

Follow the pattern as given to make Square A. The colors used for Square B are indicated in brackets.

With MC [CC2], ch 4, sl st in first ch to form ring.

RND 1: Ch 3, (counts as dc), 2 dc into ring, ch 4, work (3 dc, ch 4) into ring 3 times—12 dc total.

RND 2: Joining CC1 [CC3], ch 5 (counts as dc, ch 2), skip

scarf hoodie

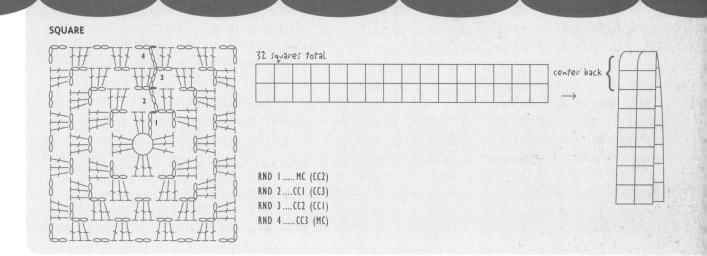

SQUARE

32 squares total

center back →

RND 1 ..... MC (CC2)
RND 2 .... CC1 (CC3)
RND 3 .... CC2 (CC1)
RND 4 ..... CC3 (MC)

first 3 dc, * work (3 dc, ch 4, 3 dc) all into ch-4 sp, ch 2, skip next 3 dc; rep from * 2 times, work (3 dc, ch 4, 2 dc) all into last ch-4 sp, sl st in 3rd ch of beg ch-3 to join.

RND 3: Joining CC2 [CC1], ch 3 (counts as dc), 2 dc in first ch-2 sp, ch 2, skip next 3 dc, * work (3 dc, ch 4, 3 dc) all into ch-4 sp, ch 2, skip next 3 dc, 3 dc into next ch-2 sp, ch 2, skip next 3 dc; rep from * 2 times, work (3 dc, ch 4, 3 dc) all into last ch-4 sp, ch 2, sl st in 3rd ch of beg ch-3.

RND 4: Joining CC3 [MC], ch 5 (counts as dc, ch 2), skip first 2 dc, * 3 dc in next ch-2 sp, ch 2, skip next 3 dc, work (3 dc, ch 4, 3 dc) all into ch-4 sp, [ch 2, skip next 3 dc, 3 dc into next ch-2 sp] twice, ch 2, skip next 3 dc; rep from * 2 times, work (3 dc, ch 4, 3 dc) all into last ch-4 sp, ch 2, 2 dc in last ch-2 sp, sl st in 3rd ch of beg ch-3.

Fasten off, leaving a long tail for sewing. Use a yarn needle to weave in ends.

Assembly

With right sides facing, sew one side of two squares together, alternating between Square A and Square B. Continue to add squares until you have one long strip of 16 squares. Make a second strip of 16 squares in the same manner. Join strips together along one long edge. Fold the scarf in half widthwise to find the center. Sew the back edge of two squares on one side of the fold to two squares on the other side of the fold to create the hood. Add fringe to both ends.

striped hat, scarf and wristband set

My good friend loves stripes. If it has a stripe in it, she wants to wear it. This matching set is sporty with a feminine flair. One important detail here is the edging on the flower—the different color makes the flower really stand out. Choose your own favorite colors for these projects, if you like. The wristbands in this set are the *pièce de résistance*. Wonder Woman did it best with her golden, bullet-proof wristbands, but this pattern gives you a chance to create some superpowers of your own. Jazz up the wristbands with different buttons and snaps or even some velcro. The 1970s would be so proud.

yarn

1 skein Cascade Yarns Cascade 220 (100% Peruvian highland wool, 220 yds ea) in color #8234 Green (MC)

1 skein each of Cascade Yarns Cascade 200 (100% Peruvian highland wool, 220 yds ea) in color #8010 Ivory (CC1), color #8412 Yellow (CC2), and color #2415 Mustard (CC3)

If making all three pieces in set, purchase two skeins of each color.

hooks and notions

size G/6 (4.50mm) hook

If necessary, change hook size to obtain gauge.

stitch marker

yarn needle

sewing needle

gauge

Hat

15 dc x 6½ rows = 4" (10cm)

Scarf

15 dc x 7 rows = 4" (10cm)

Wristband

17 dc x 7 rows = 4" (10cm)

finished sizes

Hat

22" (56cm) around x 7" (18cm) tall

Scarf

40" (102cm) long x 4" (10cm) wide

Wristband

7½" (19cm) around x 4½" (12cm) wide

notes

Please refer to the individual patterns for instructions on which rounds should be joined.

HAT

With MC, ch 4, sl st in first ch to form ring.

RND 1: Ch 3 (counts as first dc), work 12 dc into ring, place marker in last st to mark end of rnd. Do not join in first st—13 dc total.

RND 2: Work 2 dc in each st around, replace marker in last st throughout pattern—26 dc total.

RND 3: * Dc in next st, 2 dc in next st; rep from * around—39 dc total.

RND 4: * Dc in each of next 2 sts, 2 dc in next st; rep from * around—52 dc total.

RND 5: * Dc in each of next 3 sts, 2 dc in next st; rep from * around—65 dc total.

RNDS 6–11: Dc in each st around.

RND 12: Dc in each st around to last st, sl st in last st.

RND 13: Joining CC1, ch 2 (counts as hdc), hdc in each st around, sl st in 2nd ch of beg ch-2 to join.

RND 14: Joining CC2, ch 2 (counts as hdc), hdc in each st around, sl st in 2nd ch of beg ch-2 to join.

RND 15: Joining CC3, ch 2 (counts as hdc), hdc in each st around, sl st in 2nd ch of beg ch-2 to join.

RND 16: Joining MC, ch 3 (counts as dc), dc in each st around, sl st in 3rd ch of beg ch-3 to join.

RND 17: Ch 1, sc in each st around, sl st in first sc to join.

RNDS 18–19: Rep Rnd 17.
Fasten off, leaving a long tail. Use a yarn needle to weave in ends.

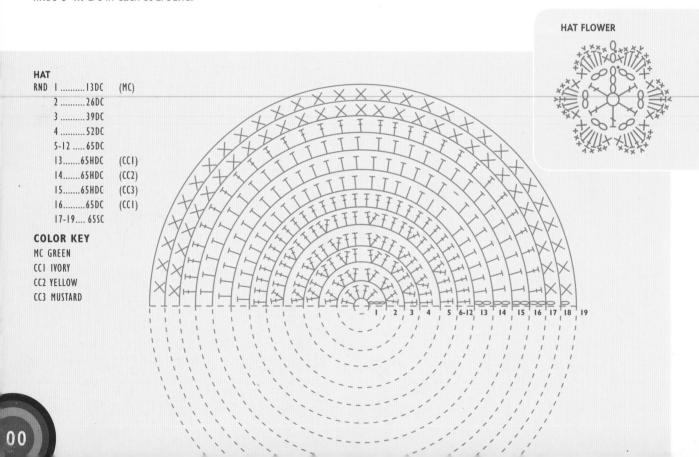

HAT FLOWER

HAT

RND 1	13 DC	(MC)
2	26 DC	
3	39 DC	
4	52 DC	
5-12	65 DC	
13	65 HDC	(CC1)
14	65 HDC	(CC2)
15	65 HDC	(CC3)
16	65 DC	(CC1)
17-19	65 SC	

COLOR KEY

MC GREEN
CC1 IVORY
CC2 YELLOW
CC3 MUSTARD

FLOWER (for Hat)

Leaving an approx 19" (48cm) tail of CC2, ch 4, sl st in first ch to form ring.

RND 1: Ch 5 (counts as dc, ch 2), work (dc, ch 2) into ring 5 times, sl st in 3rd ch of beg ch-5 to join—6 ch-2 spaces total.

RND 2: Ch 1, work (sc, 2 hdc, dc, 2 hdc, sc) into each ch-2 sp around, sl st in first sc to join—6 petals total.

RND 3: Attach CC3, ch 1, sc in same st as join, sc in each of next 2 sts, 2 sc in next st (center of petal), sc in each of next 3 sts, * sc in each of next 3 sts, 2 sc in next st, sc in each of next 3 sts; rep from * around, sl st in first sc to join.

Fasten off, leaving long tail for sewing.

FINISHING

Use the long tail and a yarn needle to sew the flower to the hat. Weave in ends.

WRISTBAND

With MC, ch 29.

ROW 1: Hdc in 3rd ch from hook and in each ch across, turn—27 hdc total.

ROW 2: Joining CC1, ch 3, dc in first st and in each st across, do not work in turning ch, turn.

ROW 3: Joining CC2, ch 3, dc in first st and in each st across, do not work in turning ch, turn.

ROW 4: Joining CC3, ch 2, hdc in first st and in each st across, do not work in turning ch, turn.

ROW 5: Joining MC, ch 2, hdc in first st and in each of next 3 sts, * 2 hdc in next st, hdc in each of next 5 sts; rep from * across, ending hdc in each of last 4 sts, do not work in turning ch, turn—31 hdc total.

ROWS 6–8: Rep Rows 2–4.

Do not fasten off.

BUTTON BAND

Turn wristband one-quarter-turn clockwise so that row ends are on top. Ch 3, dc in end of first row, work 13 dc evenly across. Sew on three evenly-spaced buttons using MC and sewing needle.

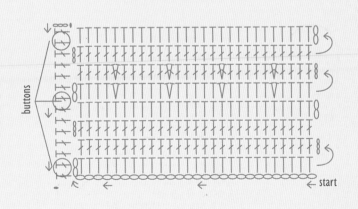

WRISTBAND

ROW 1	27HDC	(MC)
2	27DC	(CC1)
3	27DC	(CC2)
4	27HDC	(CC3)
5	31HDC	(MC)
6	31DC	(CC1)
7	31DC	(CC2)
8	31HDC	(CC3)

COLOR KEY

MC GREEN
CC1 IVORY
CC2 YELLOW
CC3 MUSTARD

buttons

← start

SCARF

With MC, ch 150.

ROW 1: Dc in 4th ch from hook and in each ch across, turn—147 dc total.

ROWS 2–4: Ch 3, dc in each st across, turn.

ROW 5: Joining CC1, ch 2, hdc in each st across, turn.

ROW 6: Joining CC2, ch 2, hdc in each st across, turn.

ROW 7: Joining CC3, ch 2, hdc in each st across, turn.
Fasten off, leaving a long tail. Use a yarn needle to weave in ends.
Add fringe to both ends of the scarf.

FLOWER (for Scarf)

With CC2, ch 4, sl st in first ch to form ring.

RND 1: Ch 5 (counts as dc, ch 2), work (dc, ch 2) into ring 5 times, sl st in 3rd ch of beg ch-5 to join—6 dc-2 spaces total.

RND 2: Ch 1, work (sc, hdc, 3 dc, hdc, sc) into each ch-2 sp around, sl st in first sc to join—6 petals total.

RND 3: Joining CC3, ch 1, sc in same st as join, sc in each of next 2 sts, 2 sc in next st (center of petal), sc in each of next 3 sts, * sc in each of next 3 sts, 2 sc in next st, sc in each of next 3 sts; rep from * around, sl st in first sc to join.

RND 4: Joining CC2, turn, work (ch 3, sl st in sp between petals) 5 times, ending ch 3, sl st in 1st ch of beg ch-3 to join.

RND 5: Turn, ch 1, work (sc, hdc, 5 dc, hdc, sc) into each ch-3 sp around, sl st in first sc to join.

RND 6: Joining CC3, ch 1, sc in same st as join, sc in each of next 2 sts, 2 sc in each of next 3 sts, sc in each of next 3 sts, * sc in each of next 3 sts, 2 sc in each of next 3 sts, sc in each of next 3 sts; rep from * around, sl st in first sc to join.

RND 7: Joining CC2, turn, work (ch 4, sl st in sp between petals) 5 times, ending ch 4, sl st in 1st ch of beg ch-4 to join.

RND 8: Turn, ch 1, work (sc, 2 hdc, 6 dc, 2 hdc, sc) into each ch-4 sp around, sl st in first sc to join.
Fasten off.

RND 9: Joining CC3, ch 1, sc in same st as join, sc in each of next 3 sts, 2 sc in each of next 4 sts, sc in each of next 4 sts, * sc in each of next 4 sts, 2 sc in each of next 4 sts, sc in each of next 4 sts; rep from * around, sl st in first sc to join.
Fasten off, leaving a long tail for sewing. Use a yarn needle to weave in ends.

BAND (for back of Flower)

Leaving an approx 10" (25cm) tail of CC2, ch 11.

ROW 1: Sc in 2nd ch from hook and in each ch across, turn—10 sc total.

ROWS 2–4: Ch 1, sc in each st across, turn.
Fasten off, leaving a long tail for sewing. Use a yarn needle to weave in ends.

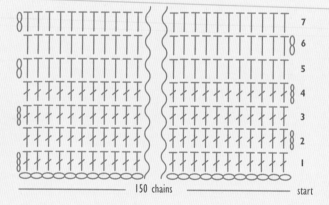

SCARF

150 chains — start

SCARF FLOWER

XXXXXXXXXX0
0XXXXXXXXXX
XXXXXXXXXX0
0XXXXXXXXXX
ooooooooooo ← start

Finishing

Slide the flower onto the scarf, then wrap the scarf around your neck and slide the free end through the loop in the back of the flower to secure the scarf.

Fringe

Cut 56 10" (25cm) strands of MC. Hold four strands together and fold them in half. Use a hook to pull the fold through the edge of the scarf at the end of each row. Pull fringe ends through the folded loop. Pull to tighten. Attach fringe to each row on both ends of scarf. Trim fringe evenly.

Flower   Hat

sew Flower onto Hat

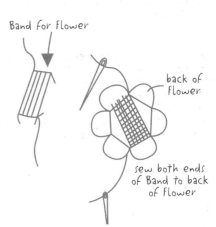

Band for Flower

back of Flower

sew both ends of Band to back of Flower

geometric earrings

This project can be made out of any extra scrap yarn. If you are a fast crocheter, you can finish a pair of earrings within fifteen minutes. Make your own personalized earrings by using different colors of crystals or lightweight beads.

Triangle Earrings

yarn

1 spool Lion Brand Lamé (metalized polyester/rayon blend, 75 yds ea) in #153 Black

hooks and notions

size C/2 (2.75mm) hook

If necessary, change hook size to obtain gauge.

4 silver jump rings

2 silver earring hooks

gauge

25 chs x 37 rows = 4" (10cm)

finished size

1¾" (5cm)

Square Earrings

yarn

1 spool Lion Brand Lamé (metalized polyester/rayon blend, 75 yds ea) in color #150 Silver

hooks and notions

size C/2 (2.75mm) hook

If necessary, change hook size to obtain gauge.

4 silver jump rings

2 silver earring hooks

2 Swarovski Crystal beads

finished size

1½" (4cm)

Flower Earrings

yarn

1 spool Lion Brand Lamé (metalized polyester/rayon blend, 75 yds ea) in color #303 Multi

hooks and notions

size C/2 (2.75mm) hook

If necessary, change hook size to obtain gauge.

4 silver jump rings

2 silver earring hooks

2 Swarovski Crystal beads

fabric glue

gauge

25 chs x 37 rows= 4" (10cm)

finished size

2" (5cm)

TRIANGLE EARRINGS (make 2)

Ch 5, sl st in first ch to form ring.

RND 1: Ch 3 (counts as dc), 2 dc into ring, (ch 5, 3 dc) into ring twice, ch 2, dc into 3rd ch of beg ch-3 to join.

RND 2: Ch 3 (counts as dc), 2 dc in sp made by joining dc, * ch 3, 3 dc in next ch-5 sp, ch 5, 3 dc in same ch-5 sp; rep from * once, ch 3, 3 dc in next ch-2 sp, ch 5, sl st in 3rd ch of beg ch-3 to join.

Fasten off and weave in ends.

SQUARE EARRINGS (make 2)

Ch 6, sl st in first ch to form ring.

RND 1: Ch 3 (counts as dc), 3 dc into ring, work (ch 3, 4 dc) into ring 3 times, ch 3, sl st in 3rd ch of beg ch-3 to join.

RND 2: Ch 2 (counts as dc), work dc dec over next 3 sts, * work (ch 3, 2-dc cluster) twice into next ch-3 sp, ch 3, dc dec over next 4 sts; rep from * 2 times, work (ch 3, 2-dc cluster) twice into last ch-3 sp, ch 3, sl st in first cluster to join.

Fasten off and weave in ends.

FINISHING

Connect two silver jump rings together. Attach one end of the jump rings to any ch-5 sp.

Attach the other end of the jump rings to the earring hook.

SQUARE EARRINGS

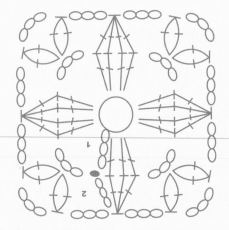

Remove 1 ch from the beg ch-3 of rnd 2. Beg dc clusters start with a ch-2.

TRIANGLE EARRINGS

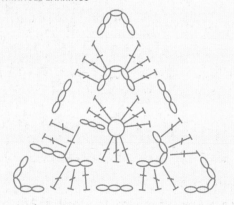

FINISHING

Connect two silver jump rings together.

Attach one end of jump rings to any corner ch-3 sp. Attach the other end of the jump rings to the earring hook. Attach a Swarovski crystal to center of each motif.

SPECIAL STITCHES

2-dc Cluster: Yo, insert hook in st, yo, pull through st, yo, pull through 2 lps on hook, yo, insert hook in same st, yo, pull through st, yo, pull through 2 lps on hook, yo, pull through all lps on hook.

dc dec: yo, insert hook in first st, yo, pull through st, yo, pull through 2 lps on hook, (yo, insert hook in next st, yo, pull through st, yo, pull through 2 lps on hook) as many times as directed, yo, pull through all lps on hook.

FLOWER EARRINGS (make 2)

Ch 6, sl st in first ch to form ring.

RND 1: Ch 1, 8 sc into ring, sl st in first sc to join.

RND 2: Ch 2 (counts as dc), dc in same st as join, * ch 4, 2-dc cluster in next st; rep from * 6 times, ch 2, hdc in first dc to join.

RND 3: Ch 1, sc in sp made by joining hdc, ch 5, * work (sc, ch 5 twice) into next ch-4 sp; rep from * around 6 times, sc into next ch-2 sp, ch 5, sl st in first sc to join.

Fasten off and weave in ends.

FLOWER EARRINGS

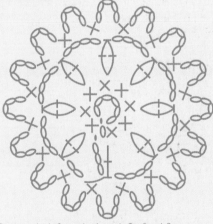

Remove 1 ch from the beg ch-3 of rnd 2.
Beg dc clusters start with a ch-2.

FINISHING

Connect two silver jump rings together. Attach one end of the jump rings to any sc between ch-5 spaces. Attach the other end of the jump rings to the earring hook. Glue a Swarovski crystal to the center of each motif.

Mr. Funky Wants You to Know

Key

- • Slip Stitch
- • Chain
- ✗ Single crochet
- T Half-double crochet
- F Double crochet

Crochet Hook Conversions

millimeter size	letter size	US number size
2.25mm	B	1
2.5mm	C	2
3mm	D	3
3.5mm	E	4
4mm	F	5
4.50mm	G	6
4.75mm		7
5mm	H	8
5.5mm	I	9
6mm	J	10
6.5mm, 7mm	K	10½
8mm	L	11
9mm	M, N	13
10mm	P	15
15mm	P, Q	
16mm	Q	
19mm	S	

Abbreviations

approx	approximately
beg	beginning
CC	contrast color
ch	chain
cont	continue
dc	double crochet
dec	decrease
foll	following
hdc	half-double crochet
MC	main color
rem	remaining
rep	repeat
RS	right side
sc	single crochet
sl st	slip stitch
sk	skip
st(s)	stitch(es)
tog	together
WS	wrong side
yo	yarn over
*	repeat

Standard Yarn Weights

1 = Superfine	2 = Fine	3 = Light	4 = Medium	5 = Bulky	6 = Super Bulky
sock, fingering, baby	sport, baby	DK, light worsted	worsted, afghan, aran	chunky, craft, rug	bulky, roving
21–32 sts	16–20 sts	12–17 sts	11–14 sts	8–11 sts	5–9 sts
2.25mm–3.5mm	3.5mm–4.5mm	4.5mm–5.5mm	5.5mm–6.5mm	6.5mm–9mm	9mm + up
B/1 to E/4	E/4 to G6	G6 to I/9	I/9 to K/10½	K/10½ to M/13	M/13 + up

The gauge given above is over 4" (10cm) of single crochet. Recommended hook sizes are given in both millimeter sizes and US number sizes.

Gauge

Gauge is simply the number of stitches and rows of a particular stitch pattern that fills a 4" (10cm) square. To create a successful project, you must match the gauge listed for the pattern. The easiest way to match gauge is to use the yarn and the size hook listed. Then crochet a 4" (10cm) square gauge swatch to make sure that your style of crochet allows you to match the listed gauge. (If you're a Nervous Nelly or a Loosey Goosey, your gauge might be different from the listed gauge because of the way you crochet.) If your gauge swatch matches up with the listed gauge, start crocheting. If it's off, try a smaller or a larger hook depending on whether your stitches are too tight or too loose.

If you're planning to use a different yarn from what's listed, you'll first want to match up the gauge on the ball band of the yarn to the listed gauge. Then, make that gauge swatch. Keep crocheting a gauge swatch until you come to the combination of yarn and hook that gives you the correct gauge. Now, for the stuffed animals in this book, gauge is not super-important. If you don't mind finding yourself with a slightly skinnier hamster or a slightly bigger bear than what's pictured, it's okay if your gauge is a little off. The same is true for the scarves. However, for the hats and mittens, gauge is definitely important. If you don't take the time and care to match it up, you'll end up with accessories that don't fit.

Check out the chart on page 108 for help in choosing yarns to substitute. The Craft Yarn Council of America has compiled a standard system for labeling yarn so it is consistent across manufacturers. Look for an image of a ball of yarn with a number on it to tell you whether a yarn is superfine, fine, light, medium, bulky or super bulky.

Basic Guide for Constructing Amigurumi Dolls

STEP ONE: Make sure to leave a long tail for each body piece.

STEP TWO: Stuff the doll's head with stuffing.

STEP THREE: Sew on the eyes, nose, ears and around nose using a darning needle and the same yarn you used to crochet the doll.

STEP FOUR: Sew the pieces of the doll together with a darning needle and the same yarn you used to crochet the doll. Make sure the parts are put together evenly.

STEP FIVE: Make the accessories and sew them to the doll if desired.

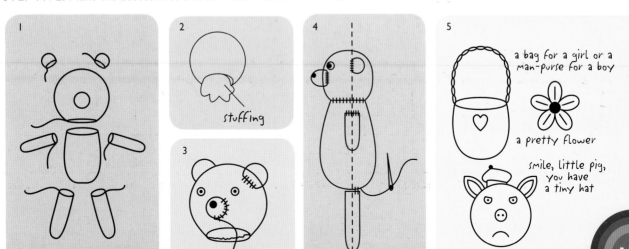

1

2

stuffing

3

4

5

a bag for a girl or a man-purse for a boy

a pretty flower

smile, little pig, you have a tiny hat

Mr. Funky's Sources

Yarn

Bernat Yarn
www.bernat.com
320 Livingstone Avenue South
Listowel, ON Canada N4W 3H3
888.368.8401

Cascade Yarns
www.cascadeyarns.com
1224 Andover Park East
Tukila, WA 98138
206.574.0440

Classic Elite
www.classiceliteyarns.com
122 Western Avenue
Lowell, MA 01851-1434
978.453.2837

Crystal Palace Yarns
www.crystalpalaceyarns.com
160 23rd St.
Richmond, CA 94804
510.237.9988

Dale of Norway
www.daleyarns.com

Lion Brand
www.lionbrand.com
135 Kero Road
Carlstadt, NJ 07072
800.258.YARN (9276)

Lily
www.sugarncream.com
320 Livingstone Avenue South
Listowel, ON Canada N4W 3H3
888.368.8401

Patons Yarns
www.patonsyarns.com
320 Livingstone Avenue South
Listowel, ON Canada N4W 3H3
888.368.8401

Red Heart
www.coatsandclark.com
Coats & Clark
PO Box 12229
Greenville, SC 29612-0229
800.648.1479

Tahki Stacy Charles Inc
www.tahkistacycharles.com
70-30 80th Street, Bldg. 36
Ridgewood, NY 11388
800.338.YARN

Crafting Supplies

American Art Clay Co., Inc
www.amaco.com
6060 Guion Road
Indianapolis, IN 46254-1222
800.374.1600
wire for cat's whiskers

Darice
www.darice.com
13000 Darice Parkway Park 82
Strongsville, OH 44149
866.432.7423
earrings and key holders, googly eyes

Fairfield
www.poly-fil.com
PO Box 1130
Danbury, CT 06813-1130
800.980.8000
stuffing

La Mode Buttons (Blumenthal Lansing co)
www.blumenthallansing.com
1929 Main Street
Lansing, IA 52151
563.538.4211
buttons for wristband

Prym Consumer USA, Inc.
www.dritz.com
PO Box 5028
Spartanburg, SC 29304
sew-on snaps for wristband

Suzusei Sogo Co., Ltd.
http://homepage3.nifty.com/suzuseieye/
1-1-5 Komagata, Taito-ku
Tokyo 111-0043, Japan
81.3.3845.2121
googly eyes

Index

Check out these other fabulous knitting and crochet titles from North Light Craft Books.

DomiKNITrix
BY JENNIFER STAFFORD

Once you know the joys of disciplined knitting, you'll never look back. Let experienced knitter Jennifer Stafford help you whip your stitches into shape. This book features a no-nonsense, comprehensive guide to essential knitting operations and finishing techniques. In the second half of the book, you'll put your knitting know-how to the test with patterns for over 20 handknit projects to wear and gift, including a halter "bra-let," a contoured zipper vest, a Jughead hat, icon sweaters and even a knitted mohawk. Plus much, much more.

ISBN-13: 978-1-58180-853-7
ISBN-10: 1-58180-853-4
flexibind vinyl, 256 pages, Z0171

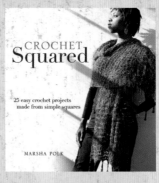

Crochet Squared
BY MARSHA A. POLK

If you can crochet a simple scarf, you can make any of the stylish and sophisticated body wraps and accessories featured in *Crochet Squared*. Each of the over 20 projects in the book is based on a simple square or rectangle shape, allowing even beginning crocheters to make gorgeous works of art. *Crochet Squared* takes crochet out of the time warp and brings it into the new millennium. Marsha Polk's striking use of color and novelty yarns makes for stunning and sophisticated projects. You'll also find a practical guide to basic crochet techniques.

ISBN-13: 978-1-58180-833-9
ISBN-10: 1-58180-833-X
paperback, 128 pages, 33507

Fitted Knits
BY STEFANIE JAPEL

Fitted Knits features 25 projects to fit and flatter. You'll learn how to tailor T-shirts, sweaters, cardigans, coats and even a skirt and a dress to fit you perfectly. Take the guesswork out of knitting garments that fit. The book includes a detailed section that shows you how to know when and where increases and decreases should be placed to create the most attractive shaping.

ISBN-13: 978-1-58180-872-8
ISBN-10: 1-58180-872-0
paperback, 128 pages, Z0574

These books and other fine North Light titles are available at your local craft or scrapbook store, bookstore or from online suppliers.